INTERNATIONAL (
GRADUATE UNI

D0806213

THE FAMILY IN MOURNING
A Guide for Health Professionals

SEMINARS IN PSYCHIATRY

Series Editor
Milton Greenblatt, M.D.

Chief, Psychiatry Service
Veterans Administration Hospital
Sepulveda, California, and
Professor of Psychiatry
University of California, Los Angeles

Other Books in Series:

THE FAMILY IN MOURNING:

A Guide for Health Professionals

Charles E. Hollingsworth, M.D.

Fellow in Pediatric Liaison Psychiatry
and Senior Child Psychiatry Fellow
UCLA Neuropsychiatric Institute
760 Westwood Plaza
Los Angeles, California 90024

Robert O. Pasnau, M.D.

Associate Professor and Chief of
Consultation Liaison Service
UCLA Neuropsychiatric Institute
Department of Psychiatry
760 Westwood Plaza
Los Angeles, California 90024

and Contributors

GRUNE & STRATTON

A Subsidiary of Harcourt Brace Jovanovich, Publishers

New York   San Francisco   London

Library of Congress Cataloging in Publication Data

Hollingsworth, Charles E.
 The family in mourning.

 (Seminars in psychiatry)
 Bibliography: p.
 Includes index.
 1. Terminal care. 2. Bereavement.
3. Psychiatric consultation. I. Pasnau, Robert O.,
joint author. II. Title.
R726.8.H64   155.9'37'02461   77-22579
ISBN 0-8089-1020-5

Grune & Stratton, Inc.
111 Fifth Avenue
New York, New York   10003

Distributed in the United Kingdom by
Academic Press, Inc. (London) Ltd.
24/28 Oval Road, London NW 1

Library of Congress Catalog Number 77-22579
International Standard Book Number 0-8089-1020-5

Printed in the United States of America

Dedicated to the memories
of our mothers

Zora M. Hollingsworth
1913–1969

Anne C. Pasnau
1905–1945

CONTENTS

Part VI. Conclusion

Contributors

Ken Carlson, Ph.D., Medical Center Rehabilitation Hospital, Department of Psychology, University of North Dakota, Box 8202, University Station, Grand Forks, North Dakota 58202

Theodore Evans, Ph.D., Department of Psychology, Pepperdine University, 8035 South Vermont Avenue, Los Angeles, California, 90044

Judith Farash, R.N., UCLA School of Nursing, 10833 Le Conte Avenue, Los Angeles, California 90024

Fawzy I. Fawzy, M.D., Assistant Professor and Associate Director of Consultation Liaison Service, UCLA Neuropsychiatric Institute, 760 Westwood Plaza, Los Angeles, California 90024

Robert Hoffman, M.D., Assistant Professor of Psychiatry in Residence, UCLA Neuropsychiatric Institute, Sepulveda Veterans Administration Hospital, 16111 Plummer Street, Sepulveda, California 91343

Cathie-Ann Lippman, M.D., Senior Child Psychiatry Fellow, UCLA Neuropsychiatric Institute, Department of Child Psychiatry, 760 Westwood Plaza, Los Angeles, California 90024

Patricia McCoy, R.N., Registered Nurse Therapist, Cardiac Rehabilitation Program, St. John's Hospital, 1328 22nd Street, Santa Monica, California 90404

Cynthia Scalzi, R.N., M.N., Clinical Nurse Specialist, UCLA Center for the Health Sciences; Lecturer, Graduate Division, UCLA School of Nursing, 10833 Le Conte Avenue, Los Angeles, California 90024

Kenneth Shine, M.D., Associate Professor of Medicine, Chief of the Division of Cardiology, UCLA Center for the Health Sciences, 10833 Le Conte Avenue, Los Angeles, California 90024

Bernice Sokol, LCSW, MSW, Supervisor, Department of Clinical Social Work, UCLA Hospitals and Clinics; Lecturer, School of Social Welfare, University of California at Los Angeles, 10833 Le Conte Avenue, Los Angeles, California 90024

David K. Wellisch, Ph.D., Assistant Professor of Medical Psychology, Department of Psychiatry, UCLA School of Medicine, 760 Westwood Plaza, Los Angeles, California 90024

Joel Yager, M.D., Associate Professor of Psychiatry, Director of Residency Education, UCLA Neuropsychiatric Institute, Department of Psychiatry, 760 Westwood Plaza, Los Angeles, California 90024

Preface

Seminars in Psychiatry presents this new work on THE FAMILY IN MOURNING for its several remarkable features:

First is the extraordinarily arresting story of a family stricken with congenital cardiopathy, trying to cope with their lethal stress. As the sword of Damocles descends on their heads, each family member responds with his or her unique coping mechanism, and the reverberations are felt by all offspring and all collaterals. The tragedy and its medical–psychological implications are discussed by all members of the professional team—the cardiologist, psychiatrist, nurse, social worker, and psychologist. Each assesses the situation and reviews in detail his particular role in management and support. This part of the book is certainly unique to the literature on death and dying.

Then, Drs. Hollingsworth and Pasnau go on to study the phenomenon of family loss in its many, many forms and contexts. The grieving spouse and the role of psychotherapy receive special treatment. The modification of the grief picture in sudden death, terminal illness, loss of children, and grief following abortion and stillbirth are sensitively reviewed. The authors' insights into the reactions of children to loss of parents are especially valuable.

The differing belief systems, rituals, and practices of various religions and sects help greatly in understanding how the patient and family background must be considered in professional efforts to provide solace and comfort. Finally, it becomes abundantly clear that before the insoluble and universal enigma of dying, all of us are children needing help and support, the medical team as well as the patients and their families.

Profound humanism and compassion, added to considerable depth of experience, make this volume a valuable contribution to the work of lightening the burden of the bereaved.

MILTON GREENBLATT, M.D.
Series Editor,
Seminars in Psychiatry.

Acknowledgments

We wish to express our appreciation to Rabbi Meyer H. Simon, D.D., Father John Collins, Gertrude Robinson, Helen Leah Fay, Dr. David Egli, and Dr. Joe Yamamoto for information on the transcultural mourning process.

Special thanks go to Ann Pearson, Margo Goldstein, and Mitzi Vogel Miller for typing the manuscripts; to Sylva Grossman for editorial assistance; to the UCLA NPI Clerical Services Department, especially Betty Romero and Eileen Dugal; and the staff of the UCLA Coronary Care Service, especially Celine Marsden, R.N., Doreen Fanning, R.N., and Cynthia Scalzi, R.N. for support throughout the project.

And finally we would like to express our gratitude to the administrative assistants who made this effort possible: Celia Brown and Sandy Lipschultz.

Introduction

Immortality

Do not stand by my grave and weep,
I am not there, I do not sleep.
I am a thousand winds that blow.
I am the diamond glints on snow.
I am the sunlight on ripened grain.
I am the gentle autumn rain.
When you awake in the morning's hush,
I am the swift upflinging rush
Of white doves in circling flight.
I am the soft starshine at night
Do not stand by my grave and cry
I am not there, I did not die.

Charles E. Hollingsworth, M.D.

Helping the dying patient and his family has long been a concern of many professions. In recent years, there has been increasing emphasis on the dying patient. This book focuses attention on the bereaved family, at times overlooked as a subject of legitimate medical responsibility. In a survey of medical schools made for the Foundation of Thanatology, Drs. Bernard Schoenberg and Arthur Carr found that about one third of all medical schools offer neither courses nor lectures on physicians' responsibilities toward families of dying patients. Yet at the same time over 500 high schools and 2000 colleges are teaching courses on death and mourning. In our book we attempt to cover many different aspects of mourning in order to make it useful to as many students as possible.

This book contains in-depth, clinical presentations which reveal the importance of a medical team approach dedicated to concern for all the medical and psycho-social aspects of the family. One section contains valuable information and advice for physicians on informing families of death in such situations as sudden death, terminal illness, the very elderly loved-one's death, and life support systems death. This section also contains information and advice to the physician for requesting autopsy permission. Several chapters are dedicated to the family in normal grief and mourning responses in such circumstances as parents' responses to the death of a family member or child, the responses of children to a death in the family, suicide in the family, a violent death, a stillbirth, the birth of a handicapped or mentally retarded child, an abortion, and an amputation of a body part. An emotional dialogue is presented in the section on the family with delayed, distorted, or prolonged grief reactions. The effect of grief and mourning in the widowed spouse is also discussed. Although not intended as a book on theory, a brief discussion of the theories of mourning is presented.

One of the most important sections for the practicing psychiatrist and psychiatric resident is the section on Helping the Helpers: The Role of Liaison Psychiatry. Here, it is our intent to describe the "model" Consultation Liaison Psychiatry Service for working with the seriously ill person, the dying patient, and the family during the stressful hospitalization, anticipatory grief, and mourning phases, as well as for working with the staff of the health care team who have become emotionally involved in the patient and his family. Those professionals who work with these families need an arena in which to discuss their feelings. Included in this section are outlines for a model liaison program for the obstetrics staff, including a workshop on the tragic birth, a program for psychiatric liaison to the bone-marrow transplant project, and a detailed description of psychosocial rounds for the coronary care unit. The interdisciplinary team approach is stressed in each chapter.

The major emphasis of this book is on helping the family in mourning. Such chapters as "The Role of Religion for Bereaved Families," "Man's Attitudes Toward Death: Funerals and Rituals," "Visiting the Family After the Death of a Loved One," and "Psychotherapy for the Bereaved," contain helpful advice and counsel. Also discussed are the cultural factors, faiths, and traditions which affect the family's reaction to sickness, death, rituals, funerals, entombment, and the process of mourning. Finally, changes in attitudes and practices of the modern American family are reviewed in the areas of funeral rituals, cremation versus burial, and the increasing cost of funerals.

We have attempted to write a book on mourning with emphasis on the entire family, a book which will investigate the many factors affecting grief and mourning. It is hoped that this will be helpful in seminars for teaching all disciplines about the family's response to dying, death, and the mourning process. The clinical presentations in this book are the dramatic materials for the discussion in later portions of the book. In fact, it was the in-depth study of the family we have named the "Lebovic family" which served as the original stimulus for writing this book. We feel that the discussion sections are more meaningful when considered in light of the human drama of the mourning process.

The helping professions are called on to assist human beings in one of life's universal crises, the one that has starkness rather than joy in its nature and many elements that are painful for us to face. Each of us, if we are engaged in helping within this crisis of death and mourning, will recognize the challenge, as perhaps in no other of life's situations, to testify to our belief in the dignity and worth of man and his family. For every family experiencing the departure of a loved one, there should be enhanced opportunity to function as a family with increased sharing, in both giving and receiving, in relationships and activities.

For every one of us as a worker, there may be the need to look more deeply at the meaning of death within the dynamics of the family, and the effect it has on them as well as on us, their supporters. Each family with which we work will increase our understanding of their feelings, their mourning experience, and their struggle to readjust. This can provide us with personal growth and competence as effective helpers. Each family experiencing death is faced with a philosophical and social dilemma, that is, their attitude toward life after death and loneliness and isolation after a death. They usually give much thought to this belief in the reality of life's ending for them here on earth in the world which they have known, whether they have viewed life with a philosophy of man as a purely finite being or seen it in the context of a belief in a continuing existence in eternity. The social dilemma is the inevitability of sensing aloneness through separation from one's fellow human beings, and especially the keenness of separation from loved ones. Thus, it is not surprising that fears, real and fantasied, conscious and unconscious, center around this experience. Nor should it be thought strange that attitudes, misconceptions, and evasions result from these fears, impeding us as we attempt to deal with this crisis. This is true of patient, family member, and whoever would be a helper in this crisis.

Experience has shown most of us how devastating and destructive separation can be if ordinary grief and mourning does not take place. The loss or severance of a treasured relationship can mean immeasurable suffering. But many of us know, too—and can be guided and strengthened by this knowledge—that separation is inherent in living and maturing. This, in turn, can make for enrichment of experience, particularly within our relationships.

Helping the dying patient and his family requires help for ourselves as helpers. The incorporation of wholesome attitudes toward self and others is a broad social responsibility to which liaison psychiatry can make a valuable contribution.

It is our deep wish that this book have a place on the shelf of each member of the health care team who has contact with the family in mourning, and that it will stimulate the interest and concern of those who do not.

Charles E. Hollingsworth, M.D.
Robert O. Pasnau, M.D.

REFERENCE

1. Fishbien M: Thanatology, looking at the doctor and the dying patient. *In* Fishbien M (ed): Dealing with Death. Med World News v. 12 no. 20 (May 21): 33, 1971

THE FAMILY IN MOURNING
A Guide for Health Professionals

PART I

The Lebovic Family: A Study in Bereavement

Charles E. Hollingsworth
and Robert O. Pasnau

1

Prologue

The 44-year-old father of six children sat silently on the sofa one evening in his usual stoic state. On this evening he suddenly said to his wife, "You better get me to the hospital. I need a doctor—my chest is being crushed." At the hospital he was noted to be short of breath and was admitted. He had a progressive downhill course of cardiomyopathy, and he was discharged and readmitted to the hospital several times during the next few months. He finally succumbed to deteriorating heart disease and pulmonary emboli. His wife was left with six children, aged three to 16. She was also left with the fear that they, too, might develop the fatal illness of their father. Her physician assured her that this was not likely to be a hereditary or familial cardiomyopathy.

One month after the husband's death, her oldest son, Alex, aged 16, began to complain of easy fatigability and shortness of breath. He spoke of his fear that he might have the same condition as his father. The family shrugged this off as impossible. His mother called the family physician who offered reassurance that it was unlikely that the disease was hereditary. He said that if she wished she could bring Alex for a physical examination and an electrocardiogram. By this time Alex felt that the family viewed him as a hypochondriac, and he refused to see the physician. He later revealed that he was frequently troubled by the fear that he would die at an early age of heart disease. Two years after the death of his father, at the age of 41, Alex's mother suffered a heart attack with cardiac arrest and successful resuscitation. Since that time she has been under medical treatment for congestive heart failure.

3

One year later, Alex, at age 19, married Debbie, the only girl he had ever dated. They were united in a double ceremony with his sister, Lana, and John, her boyfriend of two weeks. In late December during his 21st year, Alex developed a respiratory problem with shortness of breath and cough. He was given antibiotics by the family physician and was told to return to work. He soon developed symptoms of congestive heart failure and pulmonary emboli, and was admitted to the hospital. Lung scan revealed multiple pulmonary emboli. Dye studies of his legs, however, revealed no blood clots in the veins there. Cardiac catheterization and echocardiography were done, and the diagnosis of cardiomyopathy was made.[1]

When Alex's condition had stabilized and improved, the entire family was called in for a family conference. Two days before discharge from the hospital a meeting was held with the physician, primary nurse, liaison psychiatrist to the cardiology service, social worker, dietician, as well as the patient, his wife, his mother, one of his two brothers, and two of his three sisters. Alex's illness was discussed and all recommendations were explained in detail. Questions were answered by family members regarding exercise, diet, mental attitude, expected emotional stress on the patient and on the family members.

At the end of the Family Discharge Conference, Alex's wife asked to see the physician and social worker privately. She asked questions about sexual activity and discussed her desire to have a child by Alex. She wanted to become pregnant as soon as possible because she realized that her husband would probably die at an early age. She was told that it probably would be several weeks before he should engage in sexual intercourse, in no case until he was able to walk up two flights of

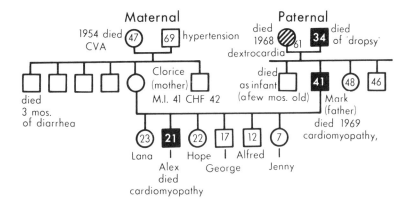

Figure 1-1. Medical family history of the Lebovic's.

steps without becoming short of breath or developing chest pain. Later, Alex's mother requested to see the social worker regarding her concern about her daughter-in-law's wanting a child.

On the afternoon following the family conference, Alex's mother collapsed at the wheel of her car and was rushed to a nearby hospital in severe respiratory distress due to congestive heart failure. She called this a "heart attack." The next morning Alex was released from his hospital and went immediately to see his mother in the Intensive Care Unit at the neighborhood hospital. She remained hospitalized for one week.

During her absence Alex did not rest as he had been instructed to do. Seven days after discharge he developed severe shortness of breath and was rushed to the neighborhood hospital's Intensive Care Unit with a diagnosis of recurrent pulmonary emboli. He died six days later. Autopsy revealed cardiomyopathy, pulmonary emboli, and pulmonary congestion.

Since that time, two of his sisters and one brother have complained of easy fatigability and shortness of breath. The mother has been particularly concerned about the oldest surviving son, George, aged 17, who had emotional problems following the death of his father five years earlier. George was arrested several times for drug abuse, delinquency, and theft. After Alex's death, George worked daily in order to buy Alex's motorcycle from Alex's wife. George also expressed the fear that he had the same type of heart disease as his father and brother.

A review of the pertinent medical family history revealed that Alex's paternal grandfather died in 1940 of "dropsy and enlarged heart" at age 34, and that his paternal grandmother died of congestive heart failure at age 61 (see Figure 1-1).

The Lebovics have a family illness, probably congenital cardiomyopathy, for which there is no known cure and which could be lurking in the genetic endowment of other members of the family.[2]

REFERENCES

1. Abbasi AS, Kattus AA: Ultrasound in the diagnosis of primary congestive cardiomyopathy. Chest 63:937–942, 1973
2. Beasley OC: Familial myocardial disease. Am J Med 29:476–485, 1960

Kenneth Shine

2

The Cardiologist's View: A Need for Long-Term Comprehensive Care

It is becoming increasingly clear in the area of critical care, although there has been a great deal said about the dying patient, that there has been little instruction and little attention to the problem of dealing with the family after the patient dies. I would emphasize this from the point of view of an internist who is responsible for training house-staff. To an intern, a death is a defeat, a moral and a scientific defeat, and if the patient had an acute illness or a potentially reversible illness, the defeat looms even larger. A medical student or young house officer can accept that a cancer patient is terminally ill. Such a death is acceptable, but to lose a patient with a myocardial infarction or heart failure, for which all kinds of therapies are available, can be an overwhelming burden. The intern's tendency is to have as little to do with the family as he can. One of his first responsibilities is to tell the family that the patient has died. That is a very difficult act in itself. The next responsibility is to ask for post-mortem permission. I suspect that there is an inverse correlation between our success in getting autopsies and the guilt that the house officer feels. Many house officers have difficulty getting autopsy permission because of the very strong feeling that to some extent they share responsibility for the bad outcome. In a major teaching institution, the house-staff then attempts to dissociate themselves from

7

the events of the day. "Get back to work, there is plenty to do. There are a lot of other sick patients. Let's work with the living." One of the processes that the physician must experience in the course of his training is a maturation of his response to death, not only in relationship to the patient but to the family. The notion that our relationship to the family as physicians, nurses, psychiatrists, and social workers cannot end with the patient's death is a fundamentally important issue. The effective family practitioner recognizes this in his continuing contacts with the family after loss of a loved one. It is an exceptional house officer who can do this. One of our major interests at the present time is an attempt to convey the notion as part of our training process.

In regard to this particular patient, his physician fell into a very easy trap. The patient was admitted to the hospital with congestive heart failure following a viral illness. A family history revealed that the father had died at age 44 of cardiomyopathy. But, because of the viral illness, his physicians implied that he had an acute viral infection which was reversible. The implication was that if he survived the acute illness he would make a complete recovery. At the time he was transferred to the Coronary Care Unit, it was my responsibility to convey to the family that he was not going to be "all right." And that, indeed, he was not going to have a very long survival. Whether the family completely believed me, a charade went on for a week or ten days, with everyone acting as if Alex were going to leave the hospital intact, and that he was going to get well because he had a viral infection. That was incorrect. On his first day in the cardiac unit it was clear that he was the sickest patient we had seen with cardiomyopathy in two years and that he was not going to survive for long. This charade the family played is a game that we play because we want to hold out hope. But when care takes on an air of unreality, it obviously compromises one's ability to help people cope with what is real.

So far as this family is concerned, once we knew that the father and son had the disease, it was clear that it was inherited as a dominant gene.[1] We now know that a third generation has the disease. The onset of symptoms in these illnesses can be very variable. A dominant gene would theoretically have a 50 percent probability of showing up in offspring.

Which of the other sibs will be affected by this disease? At what age will they develop it? It is impossible to predict which, if any, of the other children in this family may develop a cardiomyopathy in the future. Medical genetics is not able to determine if a child is a carrier for this, or if he has the dominant gene, until such time as the disease manifests itself. It is possible that one or more of these children may have inherited this cardiomyopathy, which may become apparent in their late teens or more commonly in the second or third decade of life.

We are talking about a group of diseases that affect heart muscle. The patient in heart failure is at the end stage of a variety of different kinds of disease. Inflammatory diseases, specifically viral diseases, are important causes of myocardial disease, particularly in small children. It is unclear what proportion of patients with primary diseases of the myocardium suffer them as a consequence of viral disease or by some other mechanism. Periodically a virus is implicated, but thus far no organism has been demonstrated consistently in the etiology of this group of chronic diseases.

A variety of metabolic abnormalities, including neuromuscular disorders, will produce primary myocardial disease. There is a very high incidence of hereditary disorders in this population.

We see four kinds of cardiomyopathies, all of which can be familial. In hypertrophic cardiomyopathy there is simply a thickening of the walls of the heart and initially quite normal cardiac function. The cardiac output is normal. But the eventual result is a heart in which the walls are very stiff.

Secondly, there are people who have obstructive cardiomyopathy. In this group, the enlargement of the heart is not symmetrical. The septum is adversely affected and there is obstruction between the mitral valve and the septum in this position. There is a pressure difference between the left ventricle and the aorta. Fortunately, this condition is treatable with drugs or with surgery. These obstructive cardiomyopathies may be familial.[1]

Alex's cardiomyopathy was congestive. There was an enlarged heart with a thin wall, decreased cardiac output, and increased pressures. Such patients may be short of breath, or feel weak and fatigued. They develop clots on the walls of the right or left side of the heart. Alex probably died primarily of a combination of recurrent pulmonary emboli and heart failure. He was on anticoagulants, but he had been throwing these clots either from the right ventricle, his legs, or some combination thereof.

There is a group of cardiomyopathies called restrictive, in which the wall gets very stiff because some abnormal substance is deposited there.[2] These are usually not familial. They may be due to amyloid or similar diseases.

If you look at the cardiomyopathic heart histologically you see loss of muscle cells, scar tissue formation, and sometimes inflammatory cells. In some stages the heart muscle shows vacuolation, but this is probably nonspecific, and simply indicates that the myocardial cells are degenerating. These patients have a variety of symptoms, but the most important are those caused by congestive heart failure.

A substantial number of patients with cardiomyopathy initially present have an enlarged heart, which can be seen on a chest x-ray. This may be the first sign of disease. They frequently have palpitations because they have arrhythmias; and most of the other symptoms, although significant, are less common. The hallmark of primary myocardial disease, or the cardiomyopathies, is heart failure without pain. As manifestations of heart failure, patients have shortness of breath, ankle swelling, must sit up at night to breathe, and find marked fatigue on exertion. When the disease progresses, they may develop ascites and palpitations.

Now, let's look at those cardiomyopathies which are most clearly familial. Certain childhood infiltrative diseases are familial, mainly the glycogen storage diseases and Hurler's Syndrome.[2] These children have myocardial disease, but in most of them the myocardial disease is not the predominant process in terms of their course. These are present in childhood and result from recessive genes. This means that both patients are carriers for it. There is an enormous effort to identify the presence of diseases *in utero* by the specific abnormalities which can be demonstrated in their metabolism. The liberalized abortion laws make it possible to abort fetuses found to have such glycogen storage diseases.

In the second group is a whole series of patients who have familial diseases in which there is an abnormality either the connective tissue or of the nervous system.[2] This includes Marfan's syndrome, Friedreich's ataxias and all their variants, and muscular dystrophies. All of these have high familial incidences, and cardiac disease plays a major role in the natural history of the patient. Some patients with cardiomyopathy have Wolff–Parkinson–White Syndrome and some have endocardial fibroelastosis.

From a cardiologist's point of view, there have been two major advances in the diagnosis and treatment of these cardiomyopathies.[2] One is the ability to recognize the different kinds without doing a catheterization and to follow patients with echocardiography. If a sound wave is bounced through these hearts, they can be divided into the various groups. As the heart gets bigger, the sound recording shows a bigger cavity size. As the wall of the heart gets thicker, that change can be measured. This is one of the reasons that echo studies on this family were obtained and plans made to repeat them at yearly intervals to provide early detection of a cardiomyopathy, if it should develop in any of the survivors. If researchers are going to learn anything about the natural history of the disease, the way to do it is to follow the asymptomatic children and see if observations can be made relatively early. The echocardiogram provides a sensitive way to do that.

The second important development is related to therapeutics. There is no cure for this kind of disorder, with the exception of the obstructive variety, in which you can relieve the obstruction. For the other types of cardiomyopathies, treatment is supportive. There is obviously a continuing search for toxic agents which induce cardiomyopathy. One toxic agent is alcohol. Alcohol can induce a cardiomyopathy which is reversible in its early stages if the individual stops drinking alcohol. A recent outbreak of cardiomyopathies was traced to certain beer manufacturers in Europe who discovered they got a better head on their beer by introducing cobalt, which is cardiotoxic. One must continually search for potential etiologies, since this is such a heterogeneous group of diseases. Perhaps there is a commonality of etiologies. Other than removal of known precipitating causes, particularly alcohol, and treatment of the obstructive group, everything is palliative.

Recently, patients have been treated with cardiomyopathies with a combination of nitroglycerin and Isordil.[3] This has been extremely effective with a large group of young people in their twenties who have been well maintained for prolonged periods on this particular regimen. One of the results of identifying these diseases early would be to put patients on one of these programs relatively early. We would like to be able to intervene earlier and earlier in this kind of situation by putting such patients on a prophylactic program.

Among the patients studied, Alex is the only patient who showed absolutely no response to treatment. It probably represents the severity of his disease at the time that he was examined. Indeed, it is likely that if he had been seen at age 15 or 16, perhaps it might have made some difference in his natural history. This is one of the reasons why it would be best to be able to pick up some of these other cardiomyopathies earlier in their course. For this family, it will be important to provide careful medical attention to the children and provide prompt and early treatment if symptoms of heart disease develop.

Perhaps one of the major lessons to be learned from this family is that they need a relationship with a physician which will sustain them not only through phases of health and illness, but through periods of bereavement and mourning as well.

REFERENCES

1. Emanuel R: Familial cardiomyopathies. Postgrad Med J 48:742–745, 1972
2. Freidberg CK: Diseases of the Heart. Philadelphia, Saunders, 1966, (3rd ed), pp 992–1001
3. Kovick RB, Tillish JH, Bevens SC, Bramowitz AD, Shine KI: Vasodilator therapy for chronic left ventricular failure. Circulation 53:322, 1976

Pat McCoy

3

The Nurse's Experience:
A Personal Loss

I want to take the risk of sharing some very personal things with you. I ask you to listen to my heart. Some of the things I am going to share with you will perhaps let you know why I became so involved with the Lebovic family, and especially with Alex.

I'm Pat. I'm a nurse from the Coronary Care Unit and I've worked here at the hospital for three years. I've been a registered nurse for seven years. In that time I've encountered death in many, many ways . . . in Intensive Care, in the patients on the wards, and three times in my own family. Each time, death has been a different experience for me.

When I graduated from nursing school, I told myself that I never wanted to become an uncaring, uninvolved nurse, and I hope this never happens. It is part of my own personal philosophy of nursing that it is very important to be a caring person and be able to become involved. For me to be involved with a patient is to touch them and take the risk of letting them touch me. I believe that I can be a healing nurse if I am a caring nurse. At the same time that I want this to happen, I also realize that in touching a patient at any given moment, or caring for them in any given moment, tomorrow they might not be there. But for the moment that I am with them, I want to be caring.

I had worked with coronary patients only for three months. Before that time I worked in the intensive respiratory unit. Ironically, two weeks after I began to work in the coronary care unit, I received a phone call that my own brother had died of a coronary. He was 40. He had had a myocardial infarction two years prior to this. Up until about a year ago, he had been sick from time to time, but I think I had denied that he might have been as sick as he was. I was geographically removed from him, so during the times of his illness in the past I wasn't with him. The last year of his life he had been very happy, and when I last saw him on January 1st, that was a very beautiful day for me.

Immediately before my brother's heart attack he had had the flu. He had returned to work; it was snowing; he had gone out to shovel snow. He experienced chest pain and within three hours he was gone. When I had been notified that he died I went home immediately, of course. The emotions that I first experienced were strange. I denied. Why me? I bargained, I became angry—the whole gamut of emotions. The first anger that I was able to express was the possibility that my brother had not received adequate medical care. Providing nursing care to patients who are dying is something in my nursing career that I have been involved with on a daily basis and yet I was livid with anger for a while. I found out later, of course, that he had received adequate medical care.

This time at home—it was only for five days—I experienced tremendous support and love from my family and friends.[1] My sisters were very dear to me especially, and so were my parents. I could look at my sisters and I could think, "We're all that's left." I experienced an emptiness with my brother's death that I had not experienced in death in the family prior to this. With the death of my sister-in-law and nephew it was like the emptiness that you feel when you're going down the elevator and your heart drops to your feet. But with Don, it was a vague emptiness and I washed it with tears a lot.

I came back to work the sixth day after my brother died. It was strange. I couldn't stay home any longer. I had been with the family five days and I came to work the sixth day. I was utterly exhausted, and people laughingly looked at me and a couple even said, "You look like someone just died." I was saying, "Yeah." You know, I came back to this big intellectual medical mecca, and it was amazing to me the people who were able to offer me comfort. They weren't people who could give me pious platitudes or say nice medical things, like "Well, at least he didn't suffer," or "Is there a history of heart disease in your family?" That didn't help. All I wanted people to do was reach out and touch me physically, acknowledge that I was hurting and let me hurt. Just so they knew that I was hurt. You know, he was my only brother and nothing intellectual could touch me at that point—I will never have another brother. I missed him. I wondered and I hoped that because of his death perhaps I would be able to give more to coronary patients than other people could.

Now about Alex. Alex was the age of a nephew of mine, my brother's oldest boy, who died when he was thirteen. So Alex was twenty and my nephew would have been twenty. I didn't realize this until later, but perhaps that was part of the reason that I was able to get close to Alex. I had seen Alex in the Coronary Care Unit, and I had just walked by briefly. I noticed that he seemed to be so young to be there with his long hair and his long beard. But I didn't think that much of it. When he was moved out to the floor he was there for several days. Our charge nurse asked if I would care for him, because she said he was very withdrawn and no one had been able to really reach him. So I told her I would be glad to try.

I went to Alex with an open mind and an open heart. No longer did I go to a patient and assume what the needs were and what I was going to do. Rather, I learned to be present and to learn what it was that they perceived their needs to be. To do this one has to listen and to hear what is of concern to them. At first Alex was really quiet, and I didn't know if he thought he could trust me. I had heard a lot about his personality being "very quiet," and that was really true. So I decided that if I was going to get anywhere with him I had to let him know that I really cared. How was I to show that? I went in and didn't say much. I took his vital signs. The next time I went in I let him sleep because that seemed to be what he wanted to do, especially in the mornings. I made it a point to make frequent short visits. One day when I was assigned off the ward, before going home, I made a special effort to go up to tell Alex why I hadn't seen him that day, not knowing if it would make any difference to him or not. I took care of him for about seven consecutive days. By the end of that time Alex was able to smile at me. He talked a little more. He was still very moody and depressed, and he always had the curtains closed. About two days before his discharge, I walked into the room. He was standing by the window, and the curtains were open. I pointed out to him that he seemed less depressed. He was a late sleeper. One time I asked him why he was so tired in the morning. He said it was because he never slept at night. So, for part of my nursing function one day, I sat at his bedside and tried to explore with him why he wasn't sleeping well. His simple understanding of this—he didn't think about death, that didn't keep him awake—was that those late shows he watched kept him awake. I tried to find out if there was anything about his illness that he feared. The only fear that he could verbalize to me was that he didn't want to have another one of those clots go to his lung. The major need that I heard Alex express to me was "I want to go home." Some days I did approach him with "I think you need to be taught about your medicine." So I spent some time with him along those lines. The day of discharge, I spent quite a bit of time with him and his wife. Alex could have cared less. Debbie, his wife, was very interested in what I had to say. The only thing Alex wanted to do was to go home.

One of Alex's major concerns was his potassium. He hated potassium, even to the point that he vomited a couple of times taking it. One of my nursing actions during that time was to see if I could find any way to eliminate this problem. We went through a long scene with the dietician, seeing what foods were high in potassium. The only thing that she could come up with was bananas. During our family conference, the mother asked me when I was going to get Alex a banana tree. He said that he would eat a whole bushel if it meant that he didn't have to take potassium every day.

The family's needs were very simple from my point of view, too. They seemed to appreciate being called by name. That was a very big thing to them. And eventually, when they arrived on the ward, they would look for me. All that I had done was to make an effort to find out what their names were.[1]

The family discharge conference was one of the most rewarding experiences I have had in nursing. There was such a feeling of unity and of team work. During the time I cared for Alex I don't believe that I ever dreamed how sick he really was. I heard some of the nurses saying that the doctors were talking about a heart transplant. I didn't believe this. I identified with Debbie, his wife, in that sense. I don't know if I thought he would live when he went home. Or how long he would live. I just wanted to get him there because that seemed to be what he wanted to do.

At the conclusion of our family conference, with kind of a smile on his face, (he didn't smile very much), Alex said, "I can't hide anything from them now."

Alex's mother called and left a message for me that he had died. It was interesting that the staff that I worked with were very protective. They didn't want me to get that message until they had found out the details of Alex's death. I waited about two days, and then finally one night when I was home, I decided I had to call them. I called Debbie and all I could do was cry, and say to her, "No, I didn't think he was that sick either." I just wanted her to know that I was thinking of her. When I called his mother, practically the first sentence she said to me was, "Can the other children be examined?"

The family came back for some of their interviews and they visited with me on the ward for about half an hour one day.[2] I identified with them very much. They had a tremendous need to tell me all the details of Alex's last days. Even that he shaved off his beard and that he had lost weight; that the nurses at the other hospital had a champagne party for him and Debbie on their wedding anniversary; the last things that he said—I can identify with that very much, because so often in my own mind I have gone over all the details of my brother's last words when I saw him. The day that they were there I almost shared with them that my own brother had died. But somehow I couldn't. I guess I didn't see myself in the position of wanting them to meet my needs for compassion, but I saw myself wanting to meet their needs. It was interesting, too, I felt, that the last time I had visited with the family I was beginning to detach myself from them. I felt rather strange in their presence. I felt a little uncomfortable when the mother referred to me as "Alex's nurse" to the other children in the family. At the same time, I felt a little flattered that they had identified me as such.

People give meaning to my life. I know that my experience with Alex will merge into all of my experiences in nursing, but I don't think I'll ever look at a banana and not think of Alex. And I'll never be able to care for a coronary patient and not think of my brother.

REFERENCES

1. Osborne E: When you lose a loved one. New York, Public Affairs Pamphlet No. 269, 1967, pp 1–28
2. Krant MJ: The organized care of the dying patient. Hosp Pract 7:101–108, 1972

Bernice Sokol

4

The Social Worker's View:
The History of a Family

Alex's paternal grandparents were born in Yugoslavia and came to the United States when they were very young. Alex's father, Mark Lebovic, was born in a small coal-mining town 50 miles from Pittsburgh, Pennsylvania, where his father and uncles worked in the coal mines. When Mark was five years old, his father died of "dropsy and enlarged heart" at age 34. Mark had a younger brother and sister and an older brother who died in infancy. Mark quit school in the sixth grade because of poverty and being unable to read more than his own name. Reading disability was a characteristic of all the males in the Lebovic family, which could be described as a cultural cul de sac. Mark and his brother were always employed as maintenance mechanics, while his sons were fine mechanics. Clarice began dating Mark when working as a waitress where Mark's mother was also employed in a small restaurant in a town 150 miles from Clarice's parents' home. Clarice was married to Mark after an eight month courtship when she was 18 and he was 26. She knew about Mark's childhood syncopal episodes, for which the Army had classified him ineligible for the draft. Clarice described Mark as a very quiet, stoic person who seldom spoke unless he had something important to say.

Clarice was the fourth child in a family of five children and one half brother. She also had an older brother who died in infancy. She was raised in the Catholic faith and several of her cousins were nuns.

In 1962 Clarice and Mark, with four of their children, moved from Pennsylvania to Los Angeles because of Mark's recurrent bouts of pneumonia. The two youngest children were born in Los Angeles.

The family purchased a four-bedroom house in a semi-rural area of Los Angeles. The mortgage payments were $136.00 per month including taxes, and Clarice knew that this was a good investment and planned to remain in this house. The family's income was about $538 per month from Social Security benefits, as a result of the father's death.

After Mark developed the cardiomyopathy, the children asked many questions about his illness, and when he died the children seemed not to be adequately mourning the loss, but attempted to work through their feelings by talking about him occasionally with their mother. However, they were never able to relinquish their father and remained emotionally attached to him. They remembered him as a kind, loving father who was shy in the presence of visitors, and who preferred to work on the engine of someone's car in the garage at his house. After Mark's death, Clarice began to question her Catholic religious beliefs, but she did not accept her sister-in-law's request to bring the family to Dayton, Ohio, to a faith healing tabernacle where the sister-in-law claimed to have had her own heart ailment healed.

Clarice believed that Alex was very similar to his father in many ways, especially in mechanical skills and the stoic personality. Alex dropped out of high school in his senior year and shortly thereafter was married to Debbie, a young girl who was living at their home because her parents would no longer let her live in theirs. She was the only girl Alex ever dated. Clarice described her as not being very intelligent and having difficulty in maintaining employment. Clarice didn't think that Debbie understood Alex's illness in that she thought he would get well. Her main interest was to have a child, and she hoped she was pregnant when Alex died. She was not. After Alex's death his wife would not return to the hospital for interviews or psychiatric assistance. She separated herself from his family and returned to live with her own parents.

Alex's parents did not have any special plans for their children and never forced them to do anything they did not want to do. The girls were average students in school. The boys were poor readers and spellers, but like their father they were good mechanics. The girls also demonstrated good mechanical skills.

George was the only child who posed a difficult discipline problem for Clarice. After Alfred was born, George became openly hostile and asked if he could trade Alfred for a neighbor's cat or dog. He often would ask why they had to "keep Alfred." He "just never had any use for Alfred, and to this day he pays little attention to him." When his father died, George began getting into serious trouble. He was involved in drug abuse, theft, and reckless driving. Alex had been idolized by George, who used Alex as a father surrogate as did his other brothers and sisters. After Alex's death, George had some personality changes. He began acting more maturely, but he expressed concern that he would not be able to "lead" the family as Alex had done after his father's death. It was as if George believed that he could escape from being next in line for heart disease by good behavior.

Alfred described his sister Jenny as a "picky eater." It became obvious that she was able to control the family in many situations. Jenny drew several pictures while the other family members were being evaluated (see Fig. 6-1).

Clarice described the family relationships as very pleasant and her relationship with her husband as warm, with very few quarrels or harsh words between them. They always consulted each other before making large purchases. He would give her his paycheck of about $625.00 each month, and he knew the money would be managed well. She in turn would give him $10.00 allowance. She was occasionally annoyed by his spending so much time working on cars of his various acquaintances without charging for his time. She helped support the family by working part-time driving a school bus, by working on an assembly line at General Motors, and for a short time by working as a nurse's aide at a State Mental Hospital. However, she preferred her child rearing duties at home.

One final observation was quite significant. Anniversaries and birthdays had special significance for this family. Many illnesses, deaths, and tragedies occurred on some family member's birthday or anniversary. Mark became ill the day before Easter in 1969. He died on his brother-in-law's birthday. Mark's mother was buried on his birthday in 1967 after she died of congestive heart failure just two years before he died. Clarice's brother was killed in an auto accident on another brother's birthday and was buried on a sister-in-law's birthday. Alex became ill on New Year's Eve, 1975 and died on another sister-in-law's birthday. Consequently, the family developed a marked fear and dread of anniversaries and birthdays.

The Lebovics were a family in mourning, "at risk" of severe psychosocial dysfunction.[1]

REFERENCE

1. Goldberg SB: Family tasks and reaction in the crisis of death. Soc Case-
    work 54:398–405, 1973

Theodore D. Evans

5

Psychological Assessment
of a Family in Mourning

A psychological evaluation was performed on four key family members: Clarice, and the three oldest siblings, Lana, Hope, and George. The Wechsler Adult Intelligence Scale (WAIS), the Minnesota Multiphasic Personality Inventory (MMPI), the Rorschach Ink Blot Test and selected cards from the Thematic Apperception Test were administered.

The mother's IQ score was in the dull–normal range (verbal = 92, performance = 87 for a full-scale score of 90. Throughout the testing she exhibited depressive tendencies with excessive somatic concerns. Her MMPI profile (2-6) was characteristic of an affective disorder which is typically nonpsychotic. Common complaints were sad moods, worrying, loss of initiative, and feelings of inferiority. She was seen as critical and even bitter, feeling like a victim, overburdened, mistreated, and feeling trapped. She exhibited a pervasive fear of loss of control or breaking down and therefore presented a very strong front which was designed to ward off the fear. While she did not seem to manifest an overt sense of persecution, there were indications of underlying paranoid defenses, reaction formation, and denial of anger. She often was silent, sullen, and emotionally withdrawn. This behavior was exhibited to punish family members; it also allowed some of her anger to be expressed indirectly. There were indications of an underlying thought disorder, which was apparently held in check by rather rigid defenses. These defenses resulted in a constricted, depressed, and angry individual whose ego boundaries were fragile.

Lana, her 23-year-old daughter, tested with IQ functioning in the normal range (verbal = 106, performance = 104) for a full-scale IQ score of 105. She appeared severely depressed, often to the extent of causing physiological complaints and breakdowns. The depression seemed to be long-standing. Her MMPI profile (3-1-2) suggested that many of her physical complaints were hysterical in nature. She manifested profound feelings of inferiority and uselessness and exhibited a particular difficulty in concentrating. Her performance on the Rorschach was characteristic of pervasive and long-standing repression and emotional restrictedness. There was a denial of socially unacceptable impulses, and thus, while she appeared outwardly conforming and conventional, she had many inward angry feelings the expression of which were entirely unacceptable. There were indications that she had experienced short-lived psychotic episodes which came abruptly and left quickly. Her performance on the testing could be described by the term "hysterical psychosis." However, her ego boundaries were sufficiently adequate so that she could function if her environment remained fairly constant and provided her with structure. Without this structure many of her physical complaints became rather bizarre.

In summary, Lana was an unhappy, anxious woman who dealt with the emotional impact of life through repression, was emotionally labile, and was prone to transitory psychotic states.

Hope, the 22-year-old daughter, had an IQ score of 84 (verbal = 86, performance = 83) placing her in the dull–normal range. Generally, she could be described as the healthiest in the family. There were no indications of psychosis. Rather, she was a defensive individual with an intense need to view herself in a "good light." This resulted in her denying emotional problems. On the MMPI, she had a "pure 9" profile, which is theoretically the "classic manic profile." Throughout the testing she exhibited poor inhibitory capacities which led to a "maladaptive flightiness." Significant hostility was directed at parental authority. Consequently, she may indeed have gotten into trouble in certain areas of her life where authority plays a predominant role, especially school. In order to avoid serious emotional conflict, she used various defenses, particularly escape, flight of ideas, and an over-commitment to a multitude of activities. As with the other members of this family, there was a marked inability to handle emotionality, resulting in the inordinate use of denial and significant emotional lability.

George, the 17-year-old son, had an IQ of 82 (verbal = 83, performance = 82), placing him in the dull–normal range of intelligence.

George's testing was characterized by excessive somatic concerns. There was significant emotional repression, resulting in an inability to deal with the emotional impact of the environment. Under stress, he temporarily displayed poor judgment. In an adult, his MMPI profile would suggest a psychotic diagnosis. However, many adolescents endorse deviant and bizarre items without truly being psychotic. This interpretation is supported by the high "F" scale in which he endorsed most of the deviant items and was consistent with a "cry for help" or an attempt to impress the psychologist with the severity of his condition so as to gain treatment. Outwardly, however, he maintained a rather defensive posture towards psycho-therapeutic intervention. He exhibited poor memory, immature behavior, shyness, and a flat affect throughout the testing. He strived to be overly rational as a defense against his hostile impulses and lack of inward control. There were no significant indications of psychotic thought disorder in the testing. With continued lack of intervention and family structure in this man's life, however, it could be predicted that he would experience a gradual decompensation. In summary, he was an angry, emotionally labile 17-year-old adolescent who had a very negative view of himself.

There were common personality factors running through this family system. These family members all exhibited a lack of integration of emotion into their lives. Emotionally charged material was seen as disabling. Due to this lowered capacity they all were suffering from the effects of long-term repression. They had little understanding or insight into the depth of their emotional or psychic life. Part of this lack may be seen to be an intellectual one in that they are all of low average intelligence and classic nonachievers. Emotionally, they tended to be denying, emotionally labile, disturbed individuals. The association between this hysterical style and repression is well known.[1,2] The correlation between this style and psychosomatic difficulties is also well documented.[3,4] Finally, all the members of the Lebovic family had rather weak ego boundaries which, while usually adequate to impede psychotic behavior, did result in poorly functioning defenses and depression. All were unhappy. All experienced diffuse anxiety, and all suffered from low self-esteem which further contributed to their discontent, their non-achieving, and their inability to experience normal grief and mourning.

REFERENCES

1. Alexander F: Psychosomatic Medicine. New York, Norton, 1950
2. Freud S: Fragment of an analysis of a case of hysteria. *In* The Standard Edition on the Complete Psychological Works of Sigmund Freud. London, Hogart, 1953, Vol. 7, p 7
3. Lipowski ZJ: Review of consultation psychiatry and psychosomatic medicine. I. General principles. Psychosom Med 29:153–171, 1967. II. Clinical aspects. Psychosom Med 29:201–225, 1967. III. Theoretical issues. Psychosom Med 30:395–422, 1968
4. Engel GL: Conversion symptoms. *In* MacBryde CM, Blacklow RS (eds): Sign and Symptoms. Philadelphia, Lippincott, 1970, Fifth ed., pp 650–668

Charles E. Hollingsworth
and Robert O. Pasnau

6

The Psychiatrist's Evaluation: With Sympathy

Mrs. Clarice Lebovic (Alex's mother), age 42, and her children, Lana, age 23, Hope, age 22, George, age 17, Alfred, age 12, Jenny, age 8, and one son-in-law, John Hill, age 22, the husband of Lana, appeared for a family interview a few days after Alex's death. Alex's wife, Debbie, declined to be interviewed with the family after her husband had died. In fact, she isolated herself from her husband's family and had returned to live with her own parents. John appeared to be quite disturbed by his brother-in-law's death, ostensibly because of the closeness of their relationship. At the time of the family interview it was clear that John was functioning in a psychotic manner. From the descriptions of his behavior from other family members, it was possible that he had been psychotic before Alex's death, but the death certainly exacerbated the psychotic symptoms.

Jenny, age 8, felt that she was being tested to see if her heart had the same problems as her father's and brother's. She said she had pain in her left side when running. She said that her mother had had two heart attacks and that the only funeral she had attended was Alex's. She confided that she felt he would not come back from "being dead." It was the psychiatrist's impression that Jenny was a rather inmature and narcissistic child who nonetheless was reacting to her brother's death in an appropriate way for her age. Drawings by Jenny are shown in Figure 6-1. Her self-portrait shows a child reaching up "for help from someone in the family."

Figure 6-1. Drawings by Jenny. Her self-portrait shows a child reaching up "for help from someone in the family."

Alfred, age 12, said that his father had died of heart failure because half of his heart was dead, that people go "straight up to heaven when they die," and that they come back in 100 years by reincarnation. He said that he, too, had pain in his side when running, but that it was due to breathing too hard. He remembered attending three funerals. He feared that his mother's heart "might be getting like my brother's." His mood was sad and depressed. It was the psychiatric impression that Alfred was reacting to the loss of his brother with depression, which was severe at times.

George, age 17, said that his father died when he was 12 years old, and that after that he started running with the wrong people. He admitted that he was gullible and had tried a lot of drugs, "snorted horse," was "busted for grass" and arrested for breaking and entering to steal a stereo at age 15. At age 16, the courts sent him to a camp for drug rehabilitation, where his head was shaved as a symbol of the beginning of a clean life. Three weeks after his brother Alex's death, he said the "biggest part is already over. I lost my big brother. It wasn't right. He was too young. He didn't get to enjoy life. I didn't think they would discharge him from the hospital unless he was going to be all right. While he was at home I tried to be nice to him and not get him upset. I stayed away as much as I could so I wouldn't upset him. He is probably happier now than he ever was. I don't think there is life after death. I know the doctors did the best for Alex." While Alex was in the hospital he told Debbie that he "didn't know why the doctors were wasting their time, that Alex is going to die there." George also said that he didn't have to do very much to exert himself. Sometimes when he woke up his heart pounded like it was going to rip open. He said, "I hope to die young; I don't want to be in a wheelchair or old. I try not to let my emotions show. I'm the oldest boy; I have to help them out and be available when they need someone to talk to. While I was in the camp last year, I worried about my mother's heart every day, I was so homesick. Since Alex went into the hospital I've been really short tempered and so uptight." George also admitted to being very angry at Lana's husband, John, for mistreating her. It was the psychiatric impression that George had employed antisocial acting out in response to the stress of the death of his father five years ago. There was concern that he might become even more behaviorally disturbed in response to his brother's death.

Lana Hill, Alex's sister, age 23, was worried about her marital problems with her husband, John, who had threatened to leave her since Alex's death. Her husband told her that he loved Alex and without Alex he had no reason to stay in California. He had been drinking heavily since the funeral. She was also concerned that her mother might be "becoming crazy" since Alex's death. She also was worried about her brother, George. She said the family had two things which they can say to him to hurt him. He cried when he was told by them, "Your father wouldn't like you if he saw the way you are now," and "We always wanted you to grow up to be like your father, but you are not." She felt that Alex was the only person who could communicate with George. She expressed fear of George and his friends because they were always "so redded out on downers" and they would steal from anyone. She said that at first she believed Alex was being discharged from the hospital because he was getting better. Then her mother told her the doctors were sending Alex home to die. She said, "Mom is playing on our sympathy—'Feel sorry for me—my son has died.'" When asked if she thought the heart disease was inherited, she said, "It can only be carried so far down the line if it is hereditary." She didn't think that her 11-month-old daughter had it. She did not plan

to have other children for "economic reasons." She said if it is hereditary, maybe it is only in the males. It was the psychiatric impression
that Lana was reacting to her brother's death using the neurotic defenses of denial and displacement, and that her emotional and marital
problems could intensify as a result of her brother's death.

Hope, Alex's sister, age 22, who was separated from her husband,
was concerned about the functioning of her own heart while Alex was
hospitalized. She complained of palpitations and vague chest pains,
and she saw a doctor. After Alex's death she denied having any chest
pain or palpitation and became more conerned about her youngest
brother' and sister's hearts. She stated that she had firmly believed that
Alex would be able to "live a half-way normal life" after he was
discharged from the hospital. She felt that Alex's heart disease "had to
be hereditary," but that she would still have children and hope for the
best. She said that her father had died when she was a sophomore in
high school, and that "it was a big secret that he was sick with heart
disease; the doctors didn't talk to the family. I like the way the staff at
this hospital talked to all the family." It was the psychiatric impression
that Hope seemed to be well defended against experiencing her feelings very deeply, but that her responses to both deaths in her family
were appropriate.

Clarice Lebovic, Alex's mother, said that she had had her first
heart attack at age 40, two years ago. "My heart stopped, and I thought
I had died. I could see a straight line on the monitor, and I thought I
was dead. I couldn't breath. Then I went out." She described a serious
episode of congestive heart failure one week before Alex's death. She
said that she believed that Alex's death was her fault or maybe a
combination of things. She became very tearful and said, "When his
father died, Alex told me he thought he had the same thing. He was 16,
and we just shrugged it off. Maybe if I had taken him to the doctor
then, he would have lived. I knew from the time he came in here that
he wasn't going to live. I saw him getting the same complications that
my husband had, step by step. I was trying to prepare his wife, Debbie,
for the worst. I told her he may not live. Two days before Alex died, I
dreamed that a shadow of a man handed me a card and it said, 'With
Sympathy.' I think it meant his father thought it was time for Alex to
be with him now. It meant there was going to be a death, and the only
one who was sick was Alex. When I opened the card, I woke up." She
stated that she hoped that the family would handle Alex's death as it
did his father's death, that is, by talking about him as often as possible.
She said she was riding in the car with a friend last week when he
slammed on the brakes and a toolbox in the back seat hit her on the

shoulder. She exclaimed, "I guess Alex is angry at me. That was him hitting me." She felt that the doctors sent Alex home to die. It was the psychiatric impression that Clarice Lebovic had responded to the deaths of her husband and of her son in an emotionally unstable fashion, using a combination of neurotic and borderline defenses.

The following recommendations were made to the family following the interview: Lana and her husband John were referred for marriage counseling. In addition, it was recommended that John see a psychiatrist for further evaluation and treatment. George was referred to a psychiatrist at a community Mental Health Center, but refused to go there. Mrs. Lebovic was referred to a psychiatrist for individual psychotherapy. It was hoped that she would be able to help her children after recognizing and dealing with her anger and grief.

One month after Alex's death the family was interviewed again. Jenny had cut her toe two days before the interview and insisted on riding in a wheelchair because, she said, "My doctor said to stay off that foot." Alfred expressed a great deal of jealousy of Jenny. George refused to come in and sent the message that he didn't need a psychiatrist. Lana came with her baby, and told of a dream that Alex's wife, Debbie, had tried to get in the casket with Alex, but that Alex raised up and told her that there was not room for her in his casket. Hope came and described a dream she had in which Alex returned after his funeral and said that the whole thing had been a joke on the family and that he was not dead. Clarice expressed more anger than before. She said that Alex's doctor had told her things which confused her, saying at first that the blood clots were not attached to the walls of his heart and then saying a day later that he did have blood clots in his heart. She wondered if the doctors had been keeping information from her. She also expressed animosity toward Alex's friends and family friends who had not sent flowers or sympathy cards. She had the impulse to send each of them a card signed with Alex's name and the simple inscription: With Sympathy.

Charles E. Hollingsworth
and Robert O. Pasnau

7

What We Can Learn from the Lebovic Family Experience

In *Mourning and Melancholia*, Freud examined both healthy and pathological processes of grief and described their symptoms, which were found to persist until the "work of mourning" is completed.[1] Lindemann described grief as a "definite syndrome with pathological and somatic symptomatology" which is often distorted and prolonged in the absence of psychiatric intervention, especially in male mourners. He also noted "anticipatory grief," i.e., reactions of expected death.[2]

The family responses to the death of a member may include grief, anger, guilt, turning to or away from religion, and even the wish for replacement of the dead individual. The death of a child is a tragic blow to any family, regardless of the age of the child. If the child dies in the hospital there are additional burdens, such as exhausting visits to the hospital, helpless watching while doctors attempt to save his (her) life, anxiety about the effect on other children at home, and financially devastating hospital bills. When a family member dies, the parents must cope with their own grief and help the other children in the family deal with their mourning.

In medicine there is a deep commitment to preserving life. Families with members who have serious life-threatening protracted illnesses must deal with an anticipatory mourning experience of increasing duration, intensity, and complexity. When a family member develops a life-threatening illness, the family uses a variety of psychic processes to ward off acknowledging this unendurable reality and to protect themselves from being engulfed by their anguish.

Most family members express some feelings of guilt, when a loved one dies, about the etiology of the disease, the diagnosis, delay in recognizing the initial symptoms, and treatment, such as inability to afford private treatment of superior quality.

Frequently families also express anger, and one object of their anger may be the physician who made the initial diagnosis. He is often described by them as tactless, blunt, insensitive, and incompetent. These hostile feelings do not seem to be so intense toward the doctors who treated the loved one after diagnosis. Anger at the doctor or institution is often displacement of the family members' basic anger at being singled out for such an unfortunate occurrence. Family members usually become desperate during the loved one's illness, wanting the afflicted member to be diagnosed properly and cured. After death, however, the family members are overwhelmed by guilt over what they consider to be the extra pain caused by the unsuccessful procedures. This guilt is expressed as anger toward the medical staff and institution. The hospital bill is often an emotionally laden issue if the family member has died.

The religious faith of the family is often affected by the death of a family member. For some, faith becomes stronger and religion more meaningful; for others, the inability to understand why the death occurred greatly decreases the comfort they derive from faith, and it is difficult for them to understand why they have been chosen to suffer when they have been "so good" to their families.

Many families respond to a child's death with a wish to replace him by having another child or by adopting a child. This is much more common in those families where the dead child was an only child. Some spouses find it very difficult to talk to their mate about the dead child, especially if the mate has made it clear that he or she is unwilling to talk about the dead child, in some cases to the extent of not even mentioning the dead child's name. In these cases the spouse who feels a need to talk about the dead child can do this with the other children in the family and is often comforted by their words.

Some parents, both mothers and fathers, find that separation from their living children becomes very difficult after the death of one of their children. This is experienced in different degrees by various parents ranging from initial mild anxiety after the child's death to a pathological degree where the parent cannot allow the living children to leave the home without her or him. Occassionally if there is marital conflict at the time of the death of the first newborn, the parents can focus on their marital problems and completely deny grief over the death. The death of a child is a very difficult experience for the family whether the death is relatively sudden or expected, the child is natural or adopted, or there have been previous deaths in the family.

In childhood, especially, death of a parent or sibling deprives an individual of so much opportunity to love and be loved, and in childhood a death in the family causes a difficult adjustment for the child. Mourning in children should not be compared to mourning in adults. An adult distributes his love among several meaningful relationships, such as the spouse, parents, children, friends, colleagues, as well as his work and hobbies, while a child, by contrast, invests almost all his feelings in his parents, and to a lesser extent in his siblings.

All family members do not react in the same way and, therefore, cannot be helped in the same way. The health care professional should be skilled enough to judge the pace of the individual reaction, and should be sensitive to which issues can be handled at each stage of the mourning process. During the afflicted member's illness, the health professional may talk with each one to help alleviate some of the anxieties and make the time before death as emotionally bearable as possible.

Most of the reactions and observations made in this brief discussion were confirmed in the experiences of the Lebovic family. Indeed, each family member reacted to the bereavement in the described ways, strongly influenced by the character of their personalities, the strength of their egos, and their place in the life cycle. However, in the Lebovic family, the emancipation from Mark, the husband and father, had not occurred, and the death of Alex, the father surrogate, reawakened the unresolved mourning of the father's death, which was very difficult for the family to face. In this family, we observed a group of individuals who had not worked through their earlier grief in a satisfactory manner. This had to be done before they could adequately deal with the mourning process for Alex. Each family system has its own history, its own idiosyncracies, and its unique configuration in approaching the subject of death. For this family, the special burden they had to bear was the fear of premature inevitability of death and wondering about who would be next.

The lessons learned from the Lebovic family tragedy will be repeated in further sections of this book. We feel that these lessons are most meaningful, however, when they are illustrated from our own clinical experiences, such as our work with this family.

REFERENCES

1. Freud S: Collected Papers: Mourning and Melancholia. New York, Basic Books, 1959, pp 152–150
2. Lindemann E: Symptomatology and management of acute grief. Am J Psychiatry 101:141–148, 1944

Robert O. Pasnau
and Charles E. Hollingsworth

8

Epilogue to Part I

The final chapter of the Lebovic family book is yet to be written. At the time of this writing, the family continues to face loss and uncertainty. George has developed symptoms of heart disease, but with the help he has received from several years of psychotherapy and careful medical attention prior to the onset of his illness, he has been able to cope with the demands of physical limitation and maintain good medical management. Clarice has had a stormy course with several depressions, but she is beginning to differentiate between emotional pain and the anginal pains due to her myocardial disease. She has been able to provide leadership for the family in the absence of the two strong males. Lana and her husband John did not follow through with the marriage counseling. Shortly afterwards, they separated, and he returned to his home in the middle West. The younger children are doing well emotionally, but Alfred has rather severe learning disabilities, as have all the males in the Lebovic family. They are all receiving careful periodic medical and cardiological exams. And finally, Alex's wife, Debbie, who refused all offers of assistance and help, who eventually broke all ties with her husband's family, made a serious suicidal attempt eight months after his death. She was unconscious for several days, her breathing maintained with a respirator, but due to good fortune and diligent medical care she survived without apparent brain damage. Clarice asked for us to arrange psychiatric treatment for her daughter-in-law, again assuming an important leadership role for her family. Debbie has made very good progress and has reaffirmed her close ties with Clarice, who had been like a "real mother" to her for so many years.

In facing the uncertainties of the future, the Lebovic family is stronger and better able to deal with tragedy, and they now know where to come for help. As Clarice said, ''As long as there are rainbows, I will continue to have hope.''

PART II

Informing Families of Death

Charles E. Hollingsworth
and Robert O. Pasnau

9

The Physician's Responsibility

When a patient dies, the family should be told in a sympathetic, honest, dignified, warm, and considerate manner by the physician. Some doctors have great difficulty in choosing the words to use. Others seem unable to face the task of asking for a postmortem examination, often using the rationalization that this request poses an added burden on the family at a time of crisis. Just as one would not walk out during a resuscitation, neither can this responsibility be avoided. A comfortable style and manner of meeting with families to give them this message facilitates the mourning process. It must be developed with experience and maturity.

The physician should be well organized, think about what he is going to say before he says it, and be warm and sincere. If it can be avoided, a family should never be told over the telephone that the patient has died. If the family is not at the hospital, a member of the health care team who is known to the family should call and speak to the closest relative or a designated family member. It should be communicated that the patient is in very critical condition and the doctor would like the family to assemble as soon as possible at the hospital. There should be a designated area for this purpose, preferably a family waiting room, small chapel, or any quiet room. The family should be told to drive carefully or preferably to call a taxi or a friend, *exactly* where to park the car, where to enter, where to come, and the full name of whom to contact when they arrive at the hospital.

Once the family is assembled at the hospital it is most important that they be taken to a private room so that they may be free to cry and express feelings of grief. We have found it very helpful for the members of the staff who are known to the family to be present when the family is informed that the patient has died. This group usually comprises the physician, a primary nurse, and a social worker. As many family members as possible should be seated.

It is the physician's responsibility to tell the family that their loved one has died. He should tell them the time of death and that everything was done for the patient that could have been done. It is very comforting to many families to know that. The physician should extend his sympathies to the family and then sit quietly with them for a few minutes, allowing the family members to console each other. The physician and other members of the health care team should allow the family time to cry and time to touch each other. The physician should also feel comfortable in touching the family. It has been our experience as physicians that we receive a great deal of emotional support from the other members of the health care team who accompany us on these occasions.

It should be stressed that the family be seated before the physician informs them of the death, especially any family members who are ill, elderly, or weak. The physician also should be prepared to handle syncopal episodes which sometimes occur when families are informed of the death. Patients with such syncopal episodes usually respond to being placed flat on the floor with the feet slightly higher than the head and given a brief whiff of smelling salts. However, it is important to examine carefully the person who has fainted. Some family members have been known to suffer myocardial infarctions upon receiving the news of the death of a loved one. The examination of the person who fainted or became ill should be carried out in the emergency room with the person legally registered as a patient. When possible, it should be done by an emergency room physician, allowing the physician of the deceased to be available to the other grieving family members.

After a few minutes have passed and the family appears to have accepted the initial information, the next comments should be addressed to the closest relative who has the legal responsibility for the deceased. In a forthright fashion, explain why a postmortem examination is indicated in the case of the loved one. It may be to help physicians to better understand the disease process. It may be to help make an exact diagnosis. It may be to determine if there is a hereditary disease which the family should know about. If it is a coroner's case requiring an autopsy this should be carefully explained to the family. They should be asked how they feel about the autopsy being done. Most often the families will favor an autopsy if the reasons are honestly and unhesitatingly explained to them.

Except in the coroner's case cited above, every family should be given the opportunity to decide whether or not a postmortem examination should be done on their loved one. Research has shown that many families who are not asked at the time of death decide later that if only an autopsy had been done maybe some puzzling questions could have been answered.[1] So the doctor should always use this information as part of his family conference. All hospitals are reviewed by accrediting boards. One of the indications of a high standard of medical care is a high percentage of autopsies. If this is the only reason the autopsy is being requested, the family has the right to know. If this is handled tactfully, most families will consent. It is important for the physician to remember to carry the autopsy request form with him when he goes to the family conference.

One member of the health care team should be available to the family for coordinating arrangements for a mortuary and contacting the hospital chaplain or the family's minister, priest, or rabbi. Families who are not identified with an organized religion may need considerable help from this member of the health care team in making arrangements.

Many families have experienced death previously and have learned from that experience. They can organize and make arrangements for themselves. Others may be experiencing death for the first time in their immediate family. In all cases we must remember that the death of a loved one is a crisis for the family.

The family may be too upset to make decisions. Here one must allow some flexibility. Some families cannot decide about the autopsy until the day after the death. They should be invited to return at that time to the chaplain's, nursing supervisor's, or physician's office to sign the postmortem examination request.

In the following four chapters, four vignettes are presented representing varying circumstances of death which affect the manner and style used by the physician in informing families of the death of their loved one.

REFERENCE

1. Wiseley DV: Personal communication, Los Angeles County Coroner's Office

Charles E. Hollingsworth
and Robert O. Pasnau

10

The Sudden Death

When death comes, unexpectedly and suddenly, to a family member who has been healthy and involved actively in his life, the family pain can be intense. Often, the problems of informing the families are the greatest for the emergency room physicians, who are usually tired, overworked, and have no prior relationship with the family to help them relate in a normally supportive manner. Occasionally, the physician's intense identification with a family member may either inhibit or overwhelm his ability to empathize with the family, resulting in mismanagement of the interview or no interview at all. If the death is accidental, as in the following personal account by an emergency room physician, sometimes the guilt of family members may interfere with the initiation of the normal grief process.

The ambulance pulled up to the emergency room door with sirens still screaming. A six-year-old boy had been struck by a car while crossing a street on his way home from school. He had stopped breathing enroute to the hospital. I quickly examined him and began resuscitation, but it was too late—he was dead.

The young parents arrived minutes later with a police car escort. I could hear the mother's frantic screaming in the waiting room as I covered her child's body neatly with a sheet and asked the nurse to prepare the room for me to bring in the parents. They had been seated in the family waiting room of our emergency room while I was attempting to resuscitate the child.

I walked outside and pulled a chair up in front of them and at the same time reached to take the mother's hand. "I'm sorry, he is dead," I said. The mother began to scream loudly, cry, and plead, "No, no, no, God, it can't be." The father began sobbing loudly. I sat silently, touching both of them now. The mother began saying, "Why me, why Jimmy? It can't be."

After a time the parents had pulled themselves together enough, so I said, "Would you like to view him now?" A few minutes before, the nurses had quietly signaled that the room was in order, and the resuscitation equipment had been moved to an area of the room which would not be noticeable to the parents. I held the mother's arm to support her as we walked into the room. I watched both mother and father in case they might faint; I was close enough to catch them in case they did. Fortunately, neither of them fainted. The nurse had done an excellent job of tidying the room and had washed the blood off the child's face. She had covered him with a clean sheet except for his head. The parents took a brief look—the mother kissed her hand and touched it to his forehead. The father began to sob harder. I gestured toward the door, and they came back to sit in the waiting room.

I asked if there were any family members who should be called now. All grandparents and relatives lived in another state. At this point, I suggested that the nursing supervisor who had been present for the resuscitation go with me and the parents to the quiet "chapel" across the hall from the emergency room. There I allowed the parents to sit and cry for several minutes, then I said, "It is very important that a postmortem examination be done because of the accidental death. The coroner's office will require that it be done. Do either of you have any objections to having a postmortem exam?" "No," they said quietly. I said: "It is very important that we discuss your feelings about the autopsy." They assured me that they really had no objections. I then asked them to sign the consent form for the autopsy, which they did with tear-filled eyes.

The police were waiting outside to finish their report of the accident. I left the parents with the nursing supervisor, who quietly asked the parents if they knew which mortuary they would like to use, while I explained to the police that the parents needed a few more minutes to adjust to this shock before they talked to them. I went back in to sit silently with the couple for a few more minutes, before I asked if the police could see them for a few questions. I then allowed the police to interview the parents in the chapel. I allowed the parents to use the telephone near the chapel to call relatives. Our social worker came to offer his services to the family. The family was still in disbelief—"such a tragedy—so sudden—without time to prepare."

This true account can serve as a model for discussing the problems of sudden death. In this situation the physician was the key to supporting and protecting the family. At the moment of the child's death, he recognized that his responsibility had shifted to two new patients—the child's mother and father. All of his efforts became focused upon their reactions. The importance of viewing the body and the need for privacy and expression of feelings, the legal requirements of autopsy and police reports, and the funeral arrangements were all discussed and handled with sensitivity and skill. But where does this responsibility end? What happens when this young couple leaves the emergency room?

We believe that there is need for additional medical contact with such families following the acute situation.[1] For example, we have recently seen a case in which a young child, who was under the care of an older brother while his parents were away, was killed in the street in an automobile accident. Several months later the brother was brought to the psychiatric clinic because he "wanted to die." Further exploration with the family revealed that his parents, unable to grieve probably because of their own guilt and unable to talk about the death, nonetheless blamed the sibling for his carelessness and had begun an unconscious campaign of anger and rejection directed toward him. He had already been involved in serious potentially self-destructive behavior and, without help, could be truly on a trajectory towards his own death. Such situations are by no means rare.

We believe that it is important to schedule at least one follow-up family interview for such families, ideally between two and four weeks following the tragedy. The parents should be told that they and their children are "at risk," and that early intervention can help to prevent further problems. The full account of the events leading up to the death should be discussed, and the other children should be encouraged to express their feelings, including feelings of guilt if they are present. Parents should be told how to help their children. This, we have found, makes it easier for them to deal with their own grief.

In cases such as the one in this chapter, the problem is complicated by the setting in which the physician is practicing. If he has children of his own, if he has lost a family member suddenly himself, or for any one of a dozen other reasons, he may blame his fatigue or his time pressure for not following the procedures outlined above. What this means, of course, is that it is easy to avoid what one finds unpleasant to do. Therefore, this important task must be made a part of the common practice in the emergency medical care setting.

We have found it most useful to hold several staff meetings each year in the emergency medical care unit of our hospital devoted to this topic. All staff, including physicians, nurses, and even the clerks at the front desk are included. The use of videotapes, the sharing of personal experiences, the giving of advice from senior staff, and honest presentation of the problems imposed by the physical limitations of the facility are all included in the series.

We recognize that there are no satisfactory answers to all of the problems touched upon in this chapter in the presence of so many intervening variables. Nonetheless, it is hoped that some of the above recommendations will call attention to a significant area of great need and concern for the families facing the tragedy of sudden death.

REFERENCE

1. Vollman RR, Gonzert A, Richer L, Williams WV: The reactions of family systems to sudden and unexpected death. Omega (May) 2:101–106, 1971

Charles E. Hollingsworth
and Robert O. Pasnau

11

Death Following
Terminal Illness

When one is dying there is but one question: "Have I lived well?" As Avery Weisman has noted, we do not grieve the life we have lived, but the one we might have but did not.[1] The fear of death is the understandable apprehension that one day we shall cease to be, and although we must all die, we do not all fear death to the same degree or in the same way. In the phenomenon of death, man, with all his cleverness, is powerless. He may postpone death, he may relieve its physical pains, he may rationalize away or deny its very existence, but he cannot escape it.

It has long been stated that the physician must never permit the dying patient to be deprived of hope. The Greeks said that the most horrible of ills was not to die, but to die alone. Fraternal visits have great efficacy in making the dying patient more comfortable. The patient should be treated in the warmest possible way with the touch of a handshake or the laying on of hands in some other fashion. This relieves the fear of being "untouchable" and of the dying thing being a feared object; because the touch and caress are the oldest pre-verbal means we possess of communication, solace, and comfort.

In this chapter, the patient is a 53-year-old woman who had had a mastectomy for malignant carcinoma three years previously. Unfortunately, chemotherapy had failed to halt the advancing malignancy. She and her family had met with a consulting psychiatrist on several occasions to talk about their feelings, and she had passed through stages of death and dying, including denial and isolation, anger, bargaining, depression, and acceptance; although not necessarily in that order, discussed in Dr. Elizabeth Kubler-Ross's book, *On Death and Dying*.[2]

The following personal account by the psychiatrist about the Miller family points out some of the similarities to and differences from the account in the previous chapter.

When it appeared certain that she would die within hours, her family was summoned to the hospital; her husband and her three children were with her while she was still conscious. Finally she lapsed into a coma; her husband stood on one side of her holding her hand, and two daughters stood on the other side of the bed; one held her hand, one touched her forehead, and the other sat quietly sobbing. Gradually, over a period of several minutes, her breathing became slower. One daughter came to the nurses' station and said, "Mama is going; would you call her doctor?" The nurse called me, and I quietly went into the room to be with the family while their loved one died. I had known and worked with the family through the initial phases of mourning. I felt very close to them. This death reminded me of my own mother's death. The family knew when she stopped breathing. They began to cry. I said, "She was brave, courageous, warm, and loving." I waited a few minutes, then asked if they were ready to go to the hospital chapel.

There I waited for each member of the family to be seated. Then I said, "You each have my sympathy. I hope some day we can display the courage she did. It is very important that an autopsy be done to learn more about the type and extent of cancer which your wife had, Mr. Miller. There is so much we need to learn about cancer, the type, its spread, and its response to the chemotherapy; the autopsy will help answer some of these questions. Do you have any objections to an autopsy?" He quietly replied, "None," as he began to sob harder. I handed the postmortem consent form to him and indicated where he should sign. "I believe the social worker knows the mortuary to which you want her taken?"

The oldest daughter responded positively when I said: "If you would like, I can have the social worker notify your minister also," she said "Thank you. Would you please ask her to come to the chapel to let us express our appreciation for her support during the past two months."

This case illustrates the observations of many others that even when expected, grief reactions are intense and painful. There really is no way to be totally prepared psychologically for the loss of a loved one. Yet this case shows the value of an established relationship in promoting the healing process, and the knowledge of the family that someone truly cares about them. The Miller family, too, is a family "at risk," despite all of the efforts of the consulting psychiatrist and the hospital team to help ease their sorrow. Such families should be instructed to come back for a follow-up visit from two to four weeks later to assess the nature of the grieving and provide an important monitoring and supportive function for the family. Psychiatric referral can be made at that time if the physician or other health team member feels that further evaluation or psychotherapy is indicated.

REFERENCES

1. Weisman AD: On Dying and Denying: A Psychiatric Study of Terminality. New York, Behavioral, 1972
2. Kubler-Ross E: On Death and Dying. New York, Macmillan, 1969

Charles E. Hollingsworth
and Robert O. Pasnau

12

Death with Dignity

There is dignity in the process of dying that is meaningful and significant. To this end, mankind is enhanced in the process. In this chapter, the attending physician describes the final days of a patient he had known for some time. The patient was 87 years old and lived a very active life until a stroke paralyzed her left side four years earlier. Her family had not placed her in a convalescent hospital but had lovingly cared for her at home with the help of a live-in nurse. She had been admitted to the hospital after developing congestive heart failure, pulmonary edema, and pneumonia.

The patient's daughter and son had confided in me, their mother's physician, that the family requested that no resuscitation attempt be made, since their mother had been an invalid since suffering her stroke. She had lived a happy life and would be ready to die when her time came. During her hospitalization, the family met with a psychiatrist at my recommendation in order to discuss their feelings about what should be done when their mother died. They all agreed that death with dignity would be peaceful and most acceptable under the circumstances.

Finally the time came; their mother slowly stopped breathing, her heart slowed to a weak pulse, then death. Her family surrounded her bed, watching quietly with tear-filled eyes. I, as her physician, came into the room when summoned by the nurse. I pronounced her dead and closed her eyes. I extended my sympathy to the family.

After a few minutes I asked the family to come to the hospital quiet room. They slowly filed down the corridor, supporting each other physically, and I gestured for each of them to be seated. Then I said, "She looked so peaceful at the end; I'm sure she leaves each of you with memories which will be very meaningful as you carry forth with lives as courageous as that she exemplified." I asked her daughter, "Mrs. Johnson, would you like to have an autopsy done?" "Oh, no, doctor. My mother always said she didn't want an autopsy done, and that she wanted to be buried next to my father. We want to abide by both of those requests." I turned to the family. "Is that acceptable to all of you?" I asked. "Oh, yes," they said quietly. I did not feel the need to press for an autopsy. It was not necessary. And even if the hospital had not had a good record of autopsies for accreditation purposes I would have respected the wishes of the family. "Fine. If I can be of any assistance during the next few weeks, please don't hesitate to call on me," I said. I knew that the family had already selected a mortuary and that the oldest daughter had asked the nurse to notify the mortuary.

The next day I made a phone call to the oldest daughter to offer my sympathies again and to say if anyone in the family felt the need for talking to someone, they were welcome to call me or the social worker. I reminded her that the psychiatrist was also available, and, because he had known her mother, he would be able to understand and help the family even more if any family members were experiencing any serious problems, such as depression. I went about my hospital rounds that day feeling strangely both saddened and enriched by this experienced.

Medical practice was less complicated a few years ago. The great increase of diagnostic and therapeutic methods has simplified some aspects of clinical medicine while complicating others. Whatever physicians may believe about the relative simplicity of living then and now, all will agree that dying was simpler. Forty or fifty years ago the record of a dying patient usually ended with a brief note to the effect that caffeine sodium benzoate, digitalis, and epinephrine were given terminally. Now dying patients in some hospitals are given continuous intravenous fluids, injections, drugs, artificial respiration with oxygen, and cardiac stimulation with a pacemaker. As a result it is difficult to determine whether they are alive or not. Such patients are, in effect, turned into human heart-lung preparations, much as the animals in the medical-school physiology laboratories.

We believe that any adult patient of sound mind has the right to reject any treatment proposed by his physician. In addition to this basic right, there are several valid situations which reasonably justify patients exercising this right. The first is when the anticipated benefit is not worth the suffering that it entails. The second is the event in which the treatment will not lessen the patients dependency on others or his environment, but in fact may result in more dependency than does the illness itself. The third is when the material and/or emotional cost of the treatment will impoverish those who will be his survivors without significant ultimate benefit to the patient. The fourth situation is that in which the treatment will impair what the patient considers his dignity as a human being.

Physicians have the responsibility of aiding their dying patients in making the decisions about the circumstances of their death. Treatment for the purpose of allaying discomfort must be maintained as long as the patient lives. Physicians also must take into account the need for a dying patient's remaining alive long enough to settle his affairs or to talk to some close relative whose arrival at the bedside is delayed. In all cases, the physician must keep the patient's family fully informed about his decisions and the reasons for them.

In treating terminal patients, especially cancer patients, surgically, it is well to bear in mind that some mutilating operations, although they may relieve symptoms for some time, may cause great postoperative discomfort and may make the patient ashamed of his helplessness and deformity. Such operations, even though they may be triumphs of surgical technique, should not be carried out unless the patient is fully informed of the expected surgical outcome and preferably only when effective plastic procedures can be performed subsequently to correct grotesque disfigurement.[1]

Dying patients have a right to die with comfort and dignity, and physicians must not violate this right. Implementing this is the duty of the physician. It requires no special set of regulations. Good medical practice, by aiming at maximal relief of suffering—including mental anguish—in situations in which cure is impossible secures the dying patient's right to the kind of death that he should have.[1]

In the above four situations which we have cited, only the first is concerned with the patient's physical comfort. The other three involve the right to die with dignity. In the case of Mrs. Johnson's mother, the exercise of this right provided much emotional comfort to the patient, even to her physician, and especially to her mourning family.

REFERENCE

1. MDA: The right to die with dignity. Med Sci 11(Feb. 10):202–206, 1962

Charles E. Hollingsworth
and Robert O. Pasnau

13

The Life Support Systems Death

In our time, perhaps no single issue is more controversial in the public
and medical mind than the issue of deciding at what point life begins
and when it ends. The courts have entered the process; occasionally
their decisions conflict with each other and with medical and psychiatric opinion. Religious beliefs of the patients and the physicians are also
important considerations in making the necessary decisions. The following true account by a courageous pediatrician illustrates the problems faced by physicians every day in the practice of medicine. Until
such time as society decides that medical decisions are "too important
to be left to the physicians" each physician must struggle with every
such situation in his own way.

A five-year-old girl had lapsed into a coma shortly after being admitted to
the hospital with an overwhelming staphylococcal pneumonia which had de-
stroyed her lungs due to its rapid necrotizing process. She had a respiratory
arrest, was intubated, and placed on a respirator without ever suffering cardiac
arrest.

I told her mother and father of her extremely critical condition and
guarded prognosis. They remained in a vigil in the family waiting room outside
the intensive care unit, coming in for frequent short visits, but always being
careful not to interfere with the staff's duties. Their daughter had two cardiac
arrests and was resuscitated. Chest x-rays revealed almost total lung destruction due to the huge abscesses. Her body had even begun to slowly decompose
by the fifth day, but her heart continued to beat and the respirator noisily
breathed for her.

Her electroencephalogram on three consecutive mornings showed no
cortical activity. I had met three times each day with the parents to give them
progress reports, to discuss their feelings, and to answer questions. I did not

discuss turning the respirator off. I believed that it was too great a burden to put on them in such a crisis, and I felt that the guilt from such a decision might have caused much mental turmoil in the future. I believed that this decision rested with me, who, as the physician to the entire family, could evaluate all the factors in the case. Although many physicians believe in continuing to support life by any means, at all costs, as long as there is a heartbeat, especially in such a young child, I strongly felt that it was a matter of an individual physician's conscience. I must be willing to live with my decision.

On the sixth morning, I asked the nurse to remain outside the curtained bedside. I closed the curtains and approached the child's bed. I thought for a few minutes of how my own daughter had looked when she was so young, not so many years ago. I disconnected the respirator and carefully watched her for signs of any spontaneous respiratory activity. In a few cases the patient may breath spontaneously unassisted and can be reconnected to the respirator or left to breathe unassisted; however, in this case the child did not breathe and her heart stopped beating after about two minutes. As I stood along beside her bed watching the cardiac monitor gradually slow, I felt that I had made the right decision. She was clinically dead, neurologically dead, and her body was decomposing. I could not put her parents through more of the agony, the long wait, the great expense, and the prolonged grief.

I asked the nurse to prepare the bedside area while I told the parents in the Intensive Care Waiting Room that she had died. I had hardly told them, when the mother said, "Please do an autopsy doctor; I want to know the results. I just don't understand why her body didn't have the resistance to fight off the pneumonia and why it did so much damage."

"We will arrange for the autopsy to be done as soon as possible so that it will not delay the funeral plans," I said. I handed her the autopsy consent form and indicated the place for a signature.

Her husband was still sobbing. "It seems like a long nightmare," he said. "The staff here was wonderful. The nurses have been so nice to let us be with her as much as possible in intensive care. I'm glad this wasn't a hospital with rigid rules on visiting."

I urged the family to come to my office after the autopsy results were available so that we could talk about the illness and the problems they would be facing in the future. Because this was their only child, and they were still quite young, I felt that they might want to talk about having other children. Something in the mother's insistence on the autopsy made me think that she may have been wondering if something genetic had been wrong with her daughter or if somehow she might have failed in her responsibility as a mother. In any case, this couple needed someone to talk to, as soon as possible.

Many physicians believe that the patient is dead if on three consecutive days the electroencephalogram shows no signs of life, a condition referred to as brain death.[1] With this evidence, and after the body has started to decompose, one should evaluate all the evidence, then go alone to the patient, disconnect the respirator fitting from the endotracheal tube, and determine if the patient breathes spontaneously unassisted. This responsibility should not be passed on to a nurse or anyone else. The physician should go alone to the bedside, while the family is in the waiting room and not allowed in the unit during this time. Because this decision is the physician's alone, based on his assessment of the family's feelings and of the prognosis, the physician should ask all other health care professionals to remain outside the patient's room at this time. It must be understood that all health care team professionals maintain strict confidentiality in such matters, both publicly and socially. The discontinuation of life support systems is a very sensitive subject. The well thought out act of a physician turning off a respirator could be misinterpreted by many people who would not understand the details of the case. It sounds very frightening and cold to some individuals.

It is insensitive *not* to act as the pediatrician did in the case cited above. In such cases, however, because the heavy responsibility of the physician often absorbs his momentary adaptive capacities, he may forget that for the family, the death is as traumatic and unfair as the sudden death described in Chapter 10. He may temporarily forget that his advantage lies in the relationship which has already developed with him as the physician.

In this case, the physician was alert to the parent's anxiety and asked that they return to see him. It is presumed that he helped initiate the grieving process and provided the necessary continued follow-up over the next few months as needed by the family, and that he was able to help the family decide about future children, if any, and deal with any possible guilt over the death of their beloved child.

REFERENCE

1. Voigt J: The criteria of death particularly in relation to transplantation surgery. World Med J 14:145, 1967

PART III

Observations on Mourning

Charles E. Hollingsworth
and Robert O. Pasnau

14

Parents' Reactions to the Death of their Child

Today, the death of a child seems an obscenity, a burden which parents should not be expected to bear and from which they suffer for years while relatives and friends, with their immediate sympathy, too often retreat into a defensive conspiracy of silence. Parents cannot view the death of their child as anything but hideously unnatural, and they inevitably respond with feelings of responsibility and guilt for the past agressive wishes which all parents feel at some time or other toward their children. Direct anger at the child for causing such anguish is often displaced unto the staff. This is particularly true if careful attention is not paid to the comfort-care of the dying child. Doctor Doris Howell, a noted pediatric hematologist, strongly supports all measures for pain relief in terminal pediatric cases. She states, "I have promised myself that no child in my care need die in agony."[1]

The grief of the parents bears some relationship to the age of the child, the previous health of the child, and the closeness of the relationship between the child and its parents. It takes time for parents to form attachments to their children and to develop memories and hopes and the ties of intertwined lives.

The grief syndrome results from the psychologic trauma of the death of a loved one, a trauma that invariably disrupts the psychologic and physiologic equilibrium we call health. The manifestations of grief during each state serve an important defensive function for the bereaved parent.

Ordinary grief for a parent who has lost a child can be divided into three states:

1. Shock, disbelief, and denial
2. Longing for the deceased
3. Resolution

Shock, numbness, and disbelief usually last for a period of minutes to a day or longer. In this stage is the almost universal tendency to exclaim, "Oh, no—I can't believe it," upon learning of the death. This stage seems to suggest that there is a normal human inability to accept easily or quickly the reality and finality of the separation imposed by death. It is important to remember that this numbness protects the bereaved for a time and allows him to attend to various immediate matters related to the loss. It is also important to remember that many people do not really accept that their child is dead until they see the dead body. Some parents may wail, moan, and weep, but they do so in a detached fashion devoid of any sense that this is actually happening. When this stage of shock and disbelief persists beyond several days, it is a signal that something is wrong and may provide the earliest evidence of a chronic and unyielding grief developing. Daytime sedatives and tranquilizers should be avoided in the early days of grief because such chemical calmness can artificially extend the period of numb disbelief and interfere with the natural course that grief must run.[2] Other immediate effects of bereavement for parents may include feeling abandoned, rejecting the medical facts, displaying detached calmness, exhibiting shock in the neurological sense, reacting with mania or euphoria, self-injury or accident proneness, self-blaming, and/or threatening revenge on others whom they blame for the death. The response is usually affected by a model known to be currently culturally accepted. In the impulse to project upon God, devil, self, or other human beings the blame for the death, the first response is directly dependent upon the existence of others, and, in some measure, a return to interactions with other family members. Mourning reactions and behavior by one family member will affect other family members' behavior. They may model or imitate or, on the contrary, they may set up marked reactions to compensate for one family member's intense reaction.

During the state of painful longing, the parents experience recurrent wave-like episodes of tearful longing for the child associated with thoughts, memories, or mental images of him or her. These waves are often triggered by any reminder of the child, such as a playmate's or sibling's comment, a favorite toy, a place associated with the child, or the time of day at which he returned home from school. Christmas,

Thanksgiving, and birthdays frequently provoke such episodes. These wave-like episodes tend to be especially intense and painful at night, when the distractions of the day are removed. This stage begins minutes, hours, or days after the death and reaches its peak between the second and fourth weeks. The manifestations are intense for about three months, progressively declining over the next six to twelve months.

In addition to preoccupation with memories and visual images of the deceased, about half of mourning parents have illusions of seeing or feeling the presence of the dead child. In some, this may cause a fear of insanity. For most, it is a comforting experience, offering a sense of contact with the loved one and a partial refutation of the reality of the loss. A bereaved parent may hear a door slam or a floor crack and, for a moment, believe the child is there. A strange child on the street may suddenly look startlingly like the deceased, stimulating a fleeting anticipation of reunion. In more extreme cases, this experience of the presence of the dead child takes the form of frank but transient hallucinations. Bereaved people often awaken at night with a compelling sense that the deceased is present—a dead child crying in his room or a dead teenager playing his records. The physician can help the grief-stricken by explaining that such experiences occur frequently in the course of grief and are part of the slow process of saying good-bye.

In any close relationship, there are hundreds of daily activities linked with the child. Preparing meals, getting off to school, holidays and recreational activities—all may be issues that are seriously disrupted or disorganized when the child dies. Doing these simple daily activities bring many memories of the deceased loved one.

The preoccupation with mental images of the deceased and of experiences in which the dead seem present is a function of the process of gradual adaptation to the sudden and final separation from a loved one. This ultimate, total separation is too overwhelming to comprehend or accept all at once.

During this stage, also, the following behaviors may be observed.

1. Escape or attempted escape from the conflict, through use of drugs or alcohol, moving of residence, suicide, social distractions, or work.
2. Removing all reminders of the child; deliberate forgetting or refusal to talk.
3. Perpetuation of the memory of the child or of the wish or supposed wish of the child, revenge, penance, "overdetermined" grief, religious conversion, and/or rituals of guilt.
4. Masochism, exhibition, or becoming a recluse.

5. Identification with the role of the child, or "carrying the spirit" of the child.
6. Reattachment of affections to a new child to replace the deceased loved one, or espousal of charities or causes usually related to the cause of death of the child.

Most of these behavior patterns take time and social interaction for their development. They are socially conditioned. One finds persons worrying in bereavement because their own feelings do not correspond to some preconceived or admired model or code; or accusing another member of the family of indifference because of that member's easier adjustment or more effective repression of painful emotions. In a simple culture it may be that grief is more or less sincerely standardized. The impression from current studies in our own fluxing culture is that of the amazing differences, in both the inner and outer manifestations of grief, to be observed everywhere.

Sometime between three and six months after the death, this second stage of grief begins to abate, although less manifestations may persist for as long as a year. The second stage then gradually blends into the third. During this stage of grief, the bereaved's parents progressively regain interest in the ordinary activities of their lives and in social and business relations. They continue to experience periodic episodes of sadness and painful longing and memories, but they gradually fade as each parent becomes able to remember the past and talks of the deceased child with equinimity and, eventually, with pleasure and interest. A significant number of grief-stricken parents, however, continue to feel great emptiness and sadness in their lives for more extended periods of time. The loss of a child, especially on an adolescent or young adult, may cause grief so intense that it never completely heals.

Some ways in which families have been observed to change as a result of bereavement are:

1. Redistribution of roles after the death to compensate for the change in family dynamics.
2. Development of family conflict as a consequence of incompatible role adjustments.
3. Splitting apart of family members from conflicts and jealousies.
4. Acceptance of new interpersonal responsibilities and increasing family solidarity.
5. Establishment of a new authority figure within the family.
6. Idiosyncratic reactions in accordance with the wishes of or perceived will of the deceased child.

In these ways the family in mourning gradually says good-bye. They take their sad parting, bit by bit, in a process like leaving a loved one for a long journey. The traveler embraces again until the final parting. He walks away, looks back, embracing from a distance with eyes and words of farewell. Finally, he is left only with memories. And so it is with the harsher and more final parting through death. Parents can only stand the pain of parting by means of these gradual good-byes to their memories of the child. If the pain of these waves of images and memories is avoided, the good-bye is never completed and the bereaved parent is impaired in his capacity to return his attention to the world of the living.

REFERENCES

1. Fishbien M: Dealing with death. Med World News 12(20):30–36, 1971
2. Hackett TP: Recognizing and treating abnormal grief. Hosp Physician 1 (Jan): 49–56, 1974

Charles E. Hollingsworth
and Robert O. Pasnau

15

Response of Children
to Death in the Family

A beautiful graceful yellow bird, was playing in
a lovely fountain, one day a cat was trying desperately to catch the graceful yellow bird but
could not, then a dog tried to catch the bird, but
the beautiful graceful yellow bird could out-ma-
neuver the dog and flew away; finally the bird
became weaker and weaker and eventually a
dangerous green snake came upon the bird and
killed him.

Told by a dying child, age 12

The impact of bereavement on children is very important in influencing
their development. Some psychological factors which determine the
approach for discussing this sensitive matter with such children are:
the developmental stage of the child's psychological growth, the age-
appropriate mental capacity to deal with the loss of a love object, and
the nature of the role the lost person played in the bereaved child's life.
In addition, the child's understanding of the impact of the reality and

69

circumstances of the death and what preceded it and followed it must be considered, as well as the availability of internal coping mechanisms and of environmental sources of comfort, explanation, and help in affective abreaction.

Younger siblings of the dead child react to the family disequilibrium caused by the death of the child and are especially sensitive to the mother's grief and mourning, whereas the older siblings show a capacity for independent grief that increases with age. Some children respond to the death of a sibling by wanting to talk to them in heaven and ask when the sibling will return. Older siblings may show signs of genuine grief such as sadness, loneliness, withdrawal from the family life for a time, and irritability.

In the past, the discussion of death with children was rather taboo. More recently, parents and educators have taken the view that questions a child asks about death should be answered honestly, but an effort should be made not to overwhelm the young child. In earlier times, when children were part of an adult society, they were not excluded from the problems of life and death. Death was too common to be ignored or hidden. Some of each child's brothers and sisters were very likely to die and the child himself was likely to have been at death's door before reaching adulthood.

Until 1940, the death of grownups, close friends, brothers, and sisters was experienced by young children all over the world much more commonly than it is today because of advances in medical treatment. Until two centuries ago, the death of a newborn baby was an accepted hazard of childbirth and the survival of a child beyond the first few years of life was regarded as something of a phenomenon. Rousseau, writing about the education of children in *Emile* (1762) could say "Of all the children who are born, scarcely one-half reach adolescence, and it is very likely your pupil will not live to be a man."[1] Some families named successive children after the father, so that at least one child would survive to perpetuate this name in the family. Death came frequently. Custom made some allowance for grief, but prepared everyone for inevitable loss. In the Middle Ages, the death of an infant or of a mother in childbirth was so common that it was accepted without much sorrow.

Now almost every child that is born will survive to adult life. This allows time for the development of intense and intimate psychological ties between parents and children. It is even more painful for parents today who lose children because of this more intense relationship. In addition, there is less exposure to death in the family and as a result the opportunity for discussion does not arise frequently.

Between the ages of three and five, the child can grasp the concept. During these years, as well, the child begins to struggle with his conflicts around autonomy and independent initiative. He typically feels fearful of retaliation from his parents for his intense sexual and aggressive impulses. These fears may be completely repressed, but it is not unusual for them to appear transiently as night terrors, tics, phobias, obsessions, or compulsions. Also, since magical thinking is still prevalent at this age, when misfortunes befall the preschool age child, he often identifies them as just punishment for his vivid fantasies and wishful misdeeds. Therefore, the child's response to death is heavily dependent on these psychodynamic and environmental factors.

What do children think of death—the death of others or the possible death of themselves? Of the few studies available, Furman's book *A Child's Parent Dies* is one of the best on this subject.[2] The biological reality of death and its final severance of a relationship are difficult enough for adults to comprehend. Children grasp a better understanding as their cognitive development progresses from the concrete to the abstract. Once a baby becomes aware of the existence of other people as individuals distinct from himself and distinct from objects which feed him and comfort him, he begins to be aware of loss, of the sense of absence. His idea of time is small and he cannot distinguish between short-term and long-term separation. But the realities of disappearance and reappearance are learned quickly. Parents may help children learn the difference between long- and short-term separation by the game of "peek-a-boo," which seems to be almost universal with young children. The fearful expectancy and explosive relief of a child playing "peek-a-boo" shows how real is the anxiety at possible loss. But children seem to learn very quickly to distinguish a long separation from a short one, and by the end of the first year or so a child has often learned to tolerate short separations with relative equanimity. His experience and his gradual appreciation of time sequence has helped. By this age, a child, faced with a long-term separation of a person to whom he is attached, seems to experience at least some of the features of grief and mourning shown by adults; although, of course, without the depth that memories and expectations bring.

By the time a child is two or three years old, fantasy joins hands with experience, and death takes on new dimensions of curiosity, anxiety, and fear. A child's first experience of death is likely to be in relation to his pets and his experience of death is largely affected by the feelings and reactions of the adults around him. The child soon appreciates that "dead" things have different characteristics from "live" ones. The child's emotional involvement is often very small and his parents may accept this, since their own emotional involvements is also small. Sometimes, however, parents may be shocked by their child's questions even about the death of a pet. A child has a much more dramatic grief reaction to the death of a long-time family dog than he does to the death of a recently acquired parakeet or goldfish.

The death of a grandparent, parent, or close friend is much more emotionally involved for the child, and the previous experience with death of a pet usually has not prepared the child to deal with the death of a relative or friend. When a relative or friend of the family dies, the child is very unlikely to see the body, and he is still quite likely to be told, not that the person is dead, but only that he has "gone on a journey" or "gone away" or possibly "gone up to heaven." Since the child can see that something special has happened because of the emotional upset of his family, the furtive whispering, the avoidance of direct talk, it is very important to be honest and answer the child's questions.

The child of between three and seven is not only learning facts and experiencing social attitudes about death; he also has many fantasies. Fantasy mingles with facts and with adult attitudes and adds terror to the fantasy. A child knows what it is like to hold his breath and knows what it is like to be alone. He may have dreams about suffocating or of being buried. He can imagine what it might be like to be put in a box deep in the ground, or not to be able to breathe when you are bursting with holding your breath. It might mean being alone forever.

Death for young children may also be personified. Death is what is done to you by others or by God for being bad or wicked or by an enemy who is fighting you or hates you, and it might be violent like death on television or in a movie. Most children everywhere seem to play games in which they kill each other or die violently. "Bang! Bang! You're dead!" accompanied by the certainty that the person shot really is not dead, seems to be an important way for children to deal with the fear.

In children's literature in the 1840s, death would result from disobedience, from warnings disregarded, from carelessness, or from any one of the thousand daily sins the Victorian child was taught to abjure. Modern children's literature is more carefully written in order not to frighten the child about death. If parents are too secretive and silent about discussing death with their children, they are leaving the child defenseless and vulnerable to his own fantasies.

Children can mourn and grieve at the death of a loved one, and when given an opportunity will do so unashamedly. They may be more upset by the unusual and deep emotion shown by their parents than by their actual loss. Their immediate grief may be short-lived. After some time passes, a child may begin to miss the reality of the person he knew and loved, his visits, perhaps, or his play or other aspects of his relationship, and he may then grieve and mourn for a long time. He may feel guilty for the bad thoughts he has sometimes entertained about the dead, or the death of one adult may light up his anxieties about the possible death of his own parents. If a child's sibling dies, the older child seems overwhelmed with guilt because his wishes that his younger sibling would disappear have come true. The child who is younger than the deceased sibling finds himself burdened to become the older child and to replace him. Consciously or unconsciously the child may feel that he in some way caused the person's death or that his anger or bad feelings about the person caused their death. This may lead to guilt which is often manifest in behavioral disturbances after a death in the family—nightmares, fear of leaving the home, or school phobia. If his parents are sensitive and understanding, they will give him an opportunity to show his sadness. If the child is unable to talk about what he feels so deeply he may display unexplained temper, restlessness at night, or in other ways indicate his concern about the dead person.

Children's fantasies about death make their understanding of it different from adults. We must be sensitive to the simplicity of this thought and the complexity of their emotions and fantasies if we are to talk to them about death.

The older child gradually develops a more realistic understanding of death. Grief and mourning about the death of a loved one takes on a more adult aspect as the fantasy recedes. By adolescence, his attitudes are becoming similar to those of the rest of his own family and his own culture.

The following advice was given to parents by the late Dr. Ernest Osborne, Professor of Education at Columbia University, and is reprinted here with the permission of the publisher.[3]

HELPING CHILDREN COPE WITH DEATH

One of the most challenging tasks in being a parent is that of helping children meet difficult experiences in life in ways that will help them mature and grow stronger. Being rejected by playmates, learning the difference between truth and falsehood, are some of the other more common of such difficult experiences for children.

Perhaps the most difficult problem of all is that of interpreting death to children. Fortunately, a majority of youngsters will not have direct contact with death. But there are enough of them so that it is important for parents to think through what they will say and do should someone in the family, or some friend or neighbor, die.

There are, of course, no simple, foolproof formulas that can be applied to such situations. Children and parents differ, and our own underlying feelings toward death will communicate themselves to youngsters even though we are able to say the "right" words. The parent who tries to hide his grief for the sake of the youngster will rarely be able to do so effectively. The gap between what he says and does, and the underlying feeling that the children sense, is likely to cause more confusion and distress than a straightforward expression of his deep sense of loss.

Yet, while there are no formulas, it is possible to develop some guidelines to help our youngsters face the fact of the death of someone close to them.

Children's Ideas About Death

It should be helpful, for instance, to have some picture as to the kind of ideas that children may have about death. A study made in Budapest by Maria Nagy reveals that between the ages of three and ten a child tends to pass through three different phases in his ideas about death:

The young child from age three to five denies death as a natural and final process. To him, death is like sleep: you are dead, then you are alive again; Or, as on a journey, you are gone and then you come back again. Consequently, children of this age may seem to be rather callous when they are told of the death of a member of the family. They express an immediate sorrow, but soon forget all about it, or at least give the impression of doing so.

Between ages five and nine, roughly, youngsters appear to be able to accept the idea that a particular person has died, but don't accept it as something that eventually happens to everyone—and particularly not to themselves.

Only as they reach nine or ten years of age, do they begin to recognize death as inevitable for all persons and as something that can come to them.

As with all general statements about differences in the development pattern of children, we must keep in mind that these are rough approximations. Many a child will not fit into the pattern. As a matter of fact, there are adults who, on an emotional level at least, cannot admit to themselves that death is really inevitable. Nonetheless, an understanding of the general pattern suggested by the Nagy study, and substantiated by a number of others, can be helpful as parents and physicians are faced with questions which young children raise.

An examination of some of the more common ways in which parents have tried to explain death to their youngsters should aid those of us who have not yet faced this problem. Because of their own reluctance to look at death realistically, they are likely to fall into the trap of confusing and disturbing the child even further by attempting to soften the blow. The examples cited below illustrate this problem.

1. The Davis' told five-year-old Billy on the occasion of his loved grandfather's death that the old man had gotten very tired and had gone quietly to sleep. But Billy, of course, sensed that there was something unusual and disturbing about this "sleep." For a week or more, bedtime was a trying experience. And even after Billy had been "bedded down" he was restless and distraught. It finally dawned on Mr. and Mrs. Davis that their explanation had backfired, and that their son was fighting sleep because he feared that he, too, would go off into his grandfather's kind of sleep.

2. Five-year-old Bobby Evans' grandmother, who had been his constant companion, died suddenly. The youngster's parents felt that they were protecting him by seeing to it that he had no contact with the arrangements for her burial, and only told him that grandma had gone to Long Island. In a sense, of course, they were telling him the truth, since it was there where she had been buried. But the boy showed considerable evidence of anxiety and resentment that his grandmother would have gone away without taking him with her, or at least telling him goodbye. The persistence with which he tried to find out when she would return finally forced his parents to give him a more truthful answer. To their satisfaction, although he was very sad about her death, he seemed less disturbed than when he thought she had deserted them.

It has already been pointed out that some adults, although they know better intellectually, have a feeling that the deceased husband or wife has "run out on them." Such a reaction, naturally, is likely to take place in children much more frequently. Consequently, it is important that we do whatever is necessary to allay this feeling of having been deserted. For to feel this is much more disturbing than to assimilate the fact of death.

A third kind of interpretation, not limited to homes that are avowedly religious, attributes death to God through some such statement as, "God took him," or "Jesus wanted him," or "He has gone to be an angel." As the Sherills point out in their monograph, *Interpreting*

Death to Children, parents run the risk of building in the child fear, resentment, or even hatred toward the God who, in his mind, can be the enemy who may strike down, without warning, anyone at all. This feeling, in turn, may well bring anxiety and guilt. It is true, of course, that the words we use and the tone of voice, as well as past teaching, will determine whether such a negative set of reactions develops. But it is well to keep in mind that even the "religious" explanation, about which there would seem to be no question, may well be taken by a child in quite another way than it is meant to be.

In short, the common-sense answers that usually occur to parents are not likely to be satisfactory, primarily because they are evasive. The desire to spare their children, as well as themselves, the pain of facing death realistically usually only prolongs and intensifies the disturbed feelings. It is legitimate, then, to ask what sort of an explanation is most desirable.

As has already been pointed out, there is no easy formula. In explaining the cause of death, it is necessary to deal with either accident, illness, or old age. In each instance, it is better to explain the immediate causes rather than to try to give a philosophical or religious interpretation. Rarely can the latter be understood by, or be helpful to, children. Thus, in talking about a death that has been caused by accident, the parent can emphasize the need for good judgment, care, and protecting oneself against other people's mistakes. In discussing sickness as the cause of death, parents can emphasize the lack of scientific knowledge, the need for better preventive measures, and the role of good medical care for people who are ill. In talking about old age as the contributing factor, it is well to stress the fact that everyone's body eventually grows old and tired, and that the heart can no longer do its work.

The words which one uses may be important. This is especially true in view of the fact that young children tend to personalize most of the things they think about. It should be made clear that the fact that someone has died of illness does not mean that there is a considerable chance that they, too, may soon die of that illness, or be stricken by the same kind of death-dealing accident.

Certain experiences with death will be more threatening than others. Children, one of whose playmates has died, will need extra reassurance since, naturally, they may see themselves having the same experience. The same is true when parents of children their own age are known to have died. Many a youngster has developed very real anxiety because he feels that if Johnny's father died, he can expect that this may easily happen to his own father. Often, the core of the anxiety might be expressed in the words, "What will happen to me if Father (or Mother) dies?" In light of this, one does well, after assuring the child that not many people die when they are as young as his parents, to make it quite clear what sort of arrangements would be carried out so that his life would not be too different. If the youngster knows that grandparents, uncles and aunts, or close friends of the family will be on hand to carry on, much of his anxiety is likely to be relieved.

As with adults, then, uncertainty as to what has happened and what it means is the thing that is likely to be most disturbing when death occurs. As far as the physical body is concerned, it should be made very clear that life has stopped, that the person cannot return, and that the body has been buried in a specific place. Anything short of this is apt to result in some of the kind of confusions and the misinterpretations mentioned above. The following example makes this situation clear.

Nine-year-old Arthur's father was killed in a train wreck as he was returning from work to his suburban home one evening. The shock of the sudden death, and some of her own feelings, caused his mother to arrange things so that although Arthur was told of his father's death, he was not allowed to attend the funeral. There was no discussion of the event at home. His mother thought it was better for the boy to carry on as much as possible in what she considered a normal way of life. But Arthur continued to show signs of disturbance. After talking the situation over with a neighbor, she asked the boy if he would like to see where his father was buried. His immediate positive response led her to plan a trip to the cemetery the very next day. On this trip, they were accompanied by the neighbor and her son, who was about Arthur's age. When Arthur was shown the grave, he stood for a moment and then asked, "You mean Daddy's buried under there?" When he was told that this was the case, he turned to his friend and said, "I'll beat you to the top of the hill." As the two boys raced away, his mother in a shocked tone, asked her friend, "How could he do a thing like that?" The latter was reassuring, "I think he was relieved to know what was what, and that he also needed to do something about his feelings. I'm sure you're mistaken if you think his behavior was a sign of hardheartedness and indifference. A youngster of his age can handle things by action better than through talking and thinking."

This latter point is one that is sometimes difficult for grownups to understand. Children do react very differently to death. Some seem to react at first as though nothing unusual has happened. Yet these may be the very youngsters who are most deeply affected, and who need the opportunity, tactfully presented, to talk about their feelings. Sometimes, too, children handle their feelings and develop their understanding through playing out death and funeral scenes. It is often hard for the bereaved adult to see this kind of thing. It seems to make light of what is a most poignant experience. Yet, from what we know of children and their ways of reacting, we can be gratified that they express their feelings as they do rather than locking them up inside themselves.

It has been suggested that one way in which children may be better prepared for experience with the death of a person is to have had a chance to play funeral when a pet has died, or when a wild bird's or animal body is found. Many of us probably remember the elaborate funerals which, on occasion, were a part of our play experience. Indeed, from the psychological point of view, such experiences may serve as an inoculation against some of the more violent feelings that are likely to arise when a member of the family or some other close associate dies.

But there may be certain reactions on the part of both children and grownups for which preparation is difficult. Under the emotional stress of bereavement, feelings, attitudes and behavior may crop up in ways which could scarcely have been anticipated. There was a tragic case, for example, in which the parents unwittingly made the surviving child feel he was of less significance to his parents than was the youngest child, who had tragically drowned. Grief can distort in many different ways.

There may be what Devereux has called "emotional blackmail." Youngsters may be forced into expressing a grief they do not really feel. Any tendency to carry on the usual interests and play activities is frowned upon in such a way as to make the child feel that he has committed little short of the unpardonable sin. One parent, under the pressure of his distraught feelings, expressed openly what many others may unconsciously feel, in the words, "His brother died—let him suffer, too." There is no denying that feelings of hostility may often be aroused by death. Few openly curse God or Fate, yet the hostility seeks a target, and one's own children, or the children of others, are sometimes that target.

There may also be another and continuing kind of "emotional blackmail." Fortunately, it is not too common, but it is frequent enough to deserve consideration. The deceased parent may be used as a kind of club over the child's behavior. To say, "Your father would want you to do this," or "Daddy would be very upset if he knew you were acting the way you are," years after the father's death is taking unfair advantage of the children. For there is no way in which they can check on the soundness of their mother's interpretation. And to rebel against the discipline that is rooted in the memory of their father is too disturbing to attempt openly. Nor are such tactics fair to the parent who has died. He, or she, is likely to become a kind of threatening, unsympathetic tyrant in the eyes of the child. Naturally, whether expressed or not, much feeling of hostility may grow out of this sort of use of the memory of a parent.

As is illustrated in the following, children often come to feel that in some way or other they are responsible for the death of a member of the family. Six-year-old Mary had been "shushed" a great deal during her grandfather's last days. But, understandably, at times she had forgotten and was noisy in her play. When her grandfather died, although no one had said anything that could be regarded as critical of these slips, Mary was inconsolable. Only gradually did her parents discover that she thought that grandpa would still have been alive if she had not made so much noise.

Older children, of course, are more likely to be able to talk about their feelings. But they should not be pushed into this, for they may have a need to work things out a bit inside before seeking an opportunity for expression. It is important to be ready to respond whenever they indicate their desire to talk. Parents may take the opportunity, if it seems perfectly natural, to initiate the discussion. By and large, however, it seems wiser to follow the child's lead, and surely, one should not press the issue if the child shows any reluctance to talk.

To just what extent children should participate in the funeral ceremonies of a member of the family is a debatable point. Most people seem to feel that youngsters should be spared as much as possible. A common practice is to send them away to spend time with friends when ceremonies occur. This is understandable. The adults' own feelings about death are such that they quite naturally wish to keep children from experiencing the upsetting effects that so commonly are part of funeral ceremonies. Yet, the effort to spare them is often unwise. The uncomfortable feeling that mysterious goings-on bring, the shock of being separated from the family, and the feeling that they are being shut out of something that means a great deal, may be far more disturbing than the experience of being a part of the sad and upsetting ceremonies. We have recently seen a case in which this situation occurred.

Eight-year-old Richard still remembers with sadness, and some resentment, the fact that his father did not permit him to take one last look at his mother as she lay in her casket some four years earlier. His older brothers were allowed to pay this final respect. Richard felt shut out and different, almost cheated. His father felt that such an experience would have been too upsetting for a four-year-old.

Richard's father may have been correct, but experience seems to indicate that it is usually better to err on the side of allowing the child to be part of all family experiences, rather than shutting him out from the more unpleasant ones. Naturally, there are limits. If it seems certain that, at the funeral, there will be uncontrolled behavior, it may be better to spare the child the possible ill effects of such expressions of grief. But this does not mean that he need be denied any participation. In another family with which we are acquainted, eight-year-old Ronald did not attend his grandfather's funeral, but he was asked to help serve the food that was prepared for the close friends and relatives at the family home after the services. And it seemed to mean a good deal to him to hear people talk about the fine person his grandfather had been.

Of course, there is a difference between permitting children to participate with the family and forcing them to do what the adults think they should do. There will be significant differences in feelings about participation on the part of children even in the same family.

The question, "What kind of ritual is best for children?" may be asked. There is no clear-cut answer. Generally, however, it would seem that except for protection against an uncontrollable display of emotion, they can, and should, have a part in whatever the family does in the way of honoring the dead.

In summary, the importance of permitting the younger members of the family in which death has occurred to be as much a part of the family as at other times, cannot be overemphasized. They deserve the right to "belong," to experience grief and sorrow, as well as joy and happiness. The strength derived from being close to the family during bereavement is not unlike the experiences reported from Britain during the bombings of the Second World War. In the families that remained together, though the children were exposed to greater physical dangers than were those sent out from the cities to rural areas, the children were less anxious and disturbed than were the uprooted youngsters.

In conclusion, the best advice as to the rituals best for children came from a wise and motherly woman who said: "Just take them into your arms and love them!"[3]

REFERENCES

1. Rousseau JJ: Emile. London, Everyman Library, 1963, p 62
2. Furman E: A Child's Parent Dies: Studies in Childhood Bereavement. New Haven, Conn., Yale University Press, 1974
3. Osborne E: When you lose a loved one. New York, Public Affairs Pamphlet No. 269, 1967, pp 16–28

Robert O. Pasnau
and Charles E. Hollingsworth

16

The Grieving Spouse

"You don't get over it; you get used to it."

Phyllis Silverman

When reflecting on one's own death, one naturally must consider the prospect of the sorrow and the loneliness that death is going to bring upon the spouse who survives. The ways of dying that impose the slightest ordeal on the person who dies are, by their very nature, the ways that inevitably make the shock for the survivors the severest. If a spouse suddenly dies without any signs of serious illness, there is no time for anticipating grief and the shock is very intense and painful for the widow or widower.

Milton Greenblatt has described the process in the sudden death situation. "For the grieving spouse the acute bereavement may seem like the end of the world; but it is only the beginning of a long and difficult passage from a shocking, benumbing experience of loss, hard to believe, and sometimes totally denied—to a period of relative tolerance of pain and, hopefully, in the favorable case, a new philosophical and emotional equilibrium."

All this may take years; and, in between, the widow or widower goes through hell-depression, anger, bitterness, fear, inhibition of affect, confusion, loss of initiative, increased dependency on others, and a host of other changes. Insomnia, irritability, and exacerbation of past physical and psychosomatic ailments, as well as the development of new disorders, may be in the mourner's path.[1]

The late English historian and thanatologist, Arnold Toynbee, also has written of the surviving spouse's painful experience of loss very warmly in the following passage which closes his book, *Man's Concern With Death.*

If one truly loves a fellow human being, one ought to wish that as little as possible of the pain of his or her death shall be suffered by him or by her, and that as much of it as possible should be borne by oneself. One ought to wish this, and one can, perhaps, succeed in willing it with one's mind. But can one genuinely desire it in one's heart? Can one genuinely long to be the survivor at the coming time when death will terminate a companionship that is more precious to one than one's own life is—a companionship without which one's own life would be a burden, not a boon? Is it possible for love to raise human nature to this height of unselfishness? I cannot answer this question for anyone except myself, and in my own case, before the time comes, I can only guess what my reaction is likely to be. I have already avowed a boastful guess that I shall be able to meet my own death with equanimity. I have now to avow another guess that puts me to shame. I guess that if, one day, I am told by my doctor that I am going to die before my wife, I shall receive the news not only with equanimity, but with relief. This relief, if I do feel it, will be involuntary. I shall be ashamed of myself for feeling it, and my relief will no doubt be tempered by concern and sorrow for my wife's future after I have been taken from her. All the same, I do guess that, if I am informed that I am going to die before her, a shameful sense of relief will be one element in my reaction.

My own conclusion is evident. My answer to Saint Paul's question, "O death, where is thy sting?" is Saint Paul's own answer: "The sting of death is sin." The sin that I mean is the sin of selfishly failing to wish to survive the death of someone with whose life my own life is bound up. This is selfish because the sting of death is less sharp for the person who dies than it is for the bereaved survivor.[2]

Edwin Shneidman believes that this view of Toynbee romanticizes the experience of death. He believes that the wish to survive and live as long as possible is a normal, human drive and need not be rationalized by a selfless desire to spare the spouse the pain of grief. But he does not minimize the importance and extent of the mourning process that Toynbee has described so beautifully.[3]

C. S. Lewis, in his poignant account of his grief upon the death of his wife, states the matter clearly: "I think I am beginning to understand why grief feels like suspense. It comes from the frustration of so many impulses that have become habitual. Thought after thought, feeling after feeling, action after action, had H. [his wife] for their object. Now that target is gone. I keep on through habit fitting an arrow to the string; then I remember and have to lay the bow down. So many roads lead through to H. I set out on one of them. But now there is an impossible frontier-post across it. So many roads once; now so many culs de sac."[4]

As in a war-torn area, the mourner finds that many of the familiar and taken-for-granted signposts and starting points of life are no longer there. He or she needs time to grasp the full scope of this description and rebuild.

The grieving spouse has many hard practical problems to solve: the burial, the fulfillment of the religious and cultural rites of passage expected by friends and relatives, problems related to children's anxieties and fears, financial insecurities, and the negotiation of spousal benefits and/or the processing of a complicated estate. The exhausting emotional experience leaves the bereaved person with little energy to cope with his or her life problems, let alone the needs or requirements of close dependents. Personal fears of illness and dying are aggravated; and, after the acute phase is over and the lavish expressions of affection and concern by friends and relatives quiet down, an awful burden of loneliness begins.

Socially, the bereaved is at a disadvantage, no longer fitting in well with the "circle of marrieds," but often feeling like a fifth wheel, an odd person without a proper ticket of admission to the world that counts. No wonder the trend toward tranquilizers, alcoholism, and even suicide.

Perhaps no one understands the stresses experienced by the grieving spouse better than Dr. Colin Murray Parkes, a British psychiatrist and thanatologist. In his classic study of the psychological reaction to bereavement, *The First Year of Bereavement* (published in 1970), 22 London widows under the age of 65 were studied during the 13 months after the death of their husbands. Dr. Parkes described in detail the failure of most respondents to accept warnings of the impending demise of their husbands: the occurrence of a phase of numbness as the immediate reaction to bereavement followed by a phase of yearning in which the "pangs" of grief occur, avoidance or disregard of the fact of loss, and four types of identification phenomenona. Grieving spouses had a perceptual "set" for the dead husband as well as an urge to search for him, and many experienced a restless urge toward aggressive action. Changes in anxiety and other features of grief over the course of the first year of bereavement were also mapped out in Dr. Parkes' report. The psychological and social situations of the widow 13 months after bereavement were studied also.[5]

In a separate study, Dr. Parkes followed up a total of 4486 widowers of 55 years of age and older for nine years since the death of their wives in 1957. Dr. Parkes found that of these, 213 died during the first six months of bereavement, which is 40% above the expected rate for married men of the same age. Thereafter, the mortality rate fell off gradually to that of married men and remained at the same level. Dr. Parkes found that 22.5% of the deaths were from the same diagnostic group as the wife's death, and the greatest increase in mortality during the first six months was found in the widowers dying from coronary thrombosis and other arteriosclerotic and degenerative disorders. This provides some evidence for the romanticists who for centuries have claimed that one can die from a broken heart during the early grieving period.[6]

Loss by death of a spouse has been shown to be associated with increased states of physical and mental illness and even with an increase in the mortality rate. Several studies have shown that psychological disturbances following bereavement commonly comprise atypical forms of grief, but these studies had lacked a satisfactory reference group until Dr. Parkes' studies, which concentrate on the "typical" form taken by grief.

Lindemann's anecdotal account of the reaction of 101 subjects to the death of a close friend or relative was one of the first published accounts of the reaction of bereavement. His detailed observation and clarity of description have made this a classical contribution and one of the best-known papers on this subject. He observed the following symptoms: the tendency to avoid thinking about the loss, the experiencing of somatic distress in waves, sighing, experiencing a lack of strength and exhaustion, indigestion, a sense of unreality, emotional distance from people, feelings of guilt and self-accusation, loss of warmth in relation to other people, irritability, anger, and a fear of insanity. Most important among the symptoms he described were the intense preoccupation with the image of the deceased, appearance of traits of the deceased in the behavior of the beloved, and the loss of the

normal patterns of conducting one's life.[7] These are important observations to keep in mind when one attempts to formulate ways of helping the bereaved spouse.

When working with the grieving spouse, we need experience to get
some reference point for how long the various features of grief can be
expected to last and what constitutes a pathological as opposed to a
"normal" variant of grief. Grief is a process, not a state. It is necessary to view this process sequentially as it progresses in the grieving
spouse if we are to see clearly its form and range of variation in an
unselected population.

How does the physician or other health professional begin to help
the bereaved spouse? Phyllis Silverman believes that widows themselves are the proper persons to reach out to other widows who have
not themselves necessarily asked for help. In her paper entitled "The
Widow as Caregiver in a Program of Preventive Intervention with
Other Widows," she described a program using five widows as caregivers. During a three year study, these five widows reached out to 400
new widows under the age of 60. The caregivers were themselves
widowed three years, had a high school education, and had devoted
themselves to raising children and keeping house. Although no direct
supervision was given, they talked about their experiences together
with a social worker. They were able to earn some money as a result of
their work in the program. The initial reaching out to the widows was
through a letter of introduction sponsored by religious groups. The
caregiver then visited the bereaved and left her phone number. It was
their finding that it required about three weeks before the new widow
considered herself to be a "widow." Before that time there was a
process of denial which usually precluded the acceptance of the help.
Some were initially angry at being classified as a widow and being on a
"mailing list." Some did not respond or were away when the caller
came. However, after the three-week period most looked forward to
the visit. During the early visit, the widow caregiver and widow reci-
pient most often talked about financial worries, social security problems, and other types of pensions. This was a phase of "affirmation of
life." Later on, pride and the wish to be independent posed a resistance to accepting help. Often the children became depressed. Their
performance in school declined. The widow may need help in order to
express emotion in front of her children. During this time as well the
widow usually needed a medical checkup or medication. She had to be
given permission to lean on the caregiver until she was able to function
on her own. As she went through her own personal "hell," she had to
learn to be more accepting of herself and her needs at that time.

Silverman also noted that following the problem-sharing phase, the widows needed help in learning to live as widows. Three major goals were formulated during this adaptation period: (1) She must learn to make decisions independently and unilaterally. (2) She must learn to be alone. (3) She must learn to make new friends and to be out with people. Although she may need direct advice at times when her ego is weak in the acute phase, later encouragement and support to act for herself is important. Some widows, however, tend to remain dependent and clinging and want the caregiver to substitute for the husband. This tendency may be used as a test of the degree of dependency fostered during the marriage and the ego strength of the widow. It is particularly important that the widow caregiver be available during lonely evenings, and to encourage the widow to find other single persons and other widow groups. She may also want to encourage the widow to reach out to still other widows, i.e., to become a widow caregiver herself.

In summary, the widow caregiver is a model of a grieving spouse who has lived successfully with the stigma and can function as a bridge to the community and to life itself. The caregiver has a credential by virtue of her suffering. As the widow becomes a widow caregiver, she develops a new sense of independence and worth.[8]

Some educational aids are available for setting up this program. A movie by Ed Mason entitled "Widows" may be very helpful. Phyllis Silverman has written a book for widows entitled *Helping Each Other in Widowhood*.[9] University extension programs in some of the larger cities are held in connection with the widow-to-widow program.

The authors are familiar with other widow-to-widow programs. One such program sponsored by the U.S. Navy has been extremely helpful to the widows of naval pilots during wartime. Informal programs of this type have functioned in the military service for many years. The psychiatrist or other health professional can be useful in providing consultation to groups of widows or developing group therapeutic programs for widows.

Abrahams has described a widow service line. This telephone "hot line," manned by volunteers, was developed to meet the needs of widows where personal contacts were not feasible, or perhaps even not desirable by the bereaved. The mutual self-help process was designed to be (1) informative, (2) emotionally supportive, (3) permissive of the expression of emotion, and (4) helpful with integration into society. This program was widely advertised. During one point in the program, 150 calls per day were received. It was found that the help was a mutual one. It offered opportunities for growth for both the volunteer widow caregiver and the caller. New forms of social roles were created to combat the isolation and alienation. Often, therapeutic discussions of considerable length could be carried on successfully over the telephone to benefit the bereaved person.[10]

It is important that all programs for the bereaved have some physician involvement. It must be remembered that there is an increase in the mortality rate among grieving spouses during the first year of bereavement. It has been shown that among widowers there is a 40 percent increase in mortality over the normal expectancy during the first six months of the bereavement. This most frequently occurs from heart diseases. Although it is not known how this occurs, it is believed that the intense stress of grieving causes changes in heart rate and blood pressure. There may be concommitant changes in the chemical constituents of the blood as well. It may well be that the feelings of helplessness and hopelessness are related to and responsible for precipitating the physical illness. It is therefore essential that any programs aimed at relieving the psychological stress of the grieving spouse also pay particular attention to their physical and medical needs.

It is also important that physicians and hospital staff members are aware of the importance of grief as a psychological component of illness. It must be remembered that four times as many bereaved as nonbereaved spend time in the hospital in the year following the death of their loved one. The majority of these individuals need to talk. They need help from their families, ministers, social workers, and physicians. In providing this help, the importance of the family cannot be overemphasized. As Caplan has shown, ''sub-population's influenced by support system aggregates have a lower incidence of medical-physical disease than their neighbors, especially under conditions of acute and chronic stress associated with rapid physical and social change.'' Despite the often-held belief that the current family excludes the elderly, Caplan has shown that today's family unit is still an extended one. Eighty percent of older individuals have a personal contact with at least one of their children or other member of the family during any week.[11] Thus the modern family is not necessarily a small nuclear one exclusive of the elderly. Working with the family of the bereaved has much to offer in terms of maximizing the support that these families are able to give the grieving family member.

The mourner receives considerable help from having someone to whom to ventilate deep feelings and willing to manage the most difficult and sentimental practical problems. The problem of reentry into society, of finding new interests in people, of establishing affective ties, and, hopefully, discovering a new love object are the primary therapeutic goals. It may well be that the partnership between the nonprofessional helper with unique experience in reaching the heart of the sufferer and the professional who possesses a broad training and expertise may provide the key for the development of the most effective treatment programs for the grieving spouse.

REFERENCES

1. Greenblatt M: The grieving spouse. Presented at the APA Meeting in Toronto, Canada, May 1977
2. Toynbee A: Man's Concern with Death. New York, McGraw–Hill, 1968, p 43
3. Shneidman ES: Deaths of Man. New York, Quadrangle/New York Times, 1973
4. Lewis CA: A Grief Observed. New York, Seabury, 1963
5. Parkes CM: The first year of bereavement. Psychiatry 33: 444–467, 1970
6. Parkes CM: The effects of bereavement on physical and mental health: a study of the case records of widows. Med J 2:274–279, 1964
7. Lindemann E: Symptomatology and management of acute grief. Psychiatry 101(2):141–148, 1944
8. Silverman PR: The widow as caregiver in a program of preventive intervention with other widows. *In* Caplan G, Killilea M (eds.): Support Systems and Mutual Help. New York, Grune & Stratton, 1976
9. Silverman PR: Helping each other in widowhood. New York, Health Science, 1974
10. Abrahams RB: Mutual helping: Styles of caregiving in a mutual aid program—the widowed service line. *In* Caplan G, Killilea M (eds): Support Systems and Mutual Help. New York, Grune & Stratton, 1976
11. Caplan G: The family as a support system. In Caplan G, Killilea M (eds): Support Systems and Mutual Help. New York, Grune & Stratton, 1976

Robert O. Pasnau
and Judith L. Farash

17

Loss and Mourning
After Abortion

Within the past decade, the practice of abortion has become more commonly accepted and is done with conditional legal approval in the United States, Japan, many countries in Europe, and the rest of the world. In many localities, termination of pregnancy is performed upon request of the woman, in contrast to the prior practice which required medical sanction.

Some attention has been directed toward the emotional needs of the women and the emotional consequences of abortion. To date, these studies have failed to demonstrate any significant long-term psychiatric sequellae to abortion in most women. However, the studies do not differentiate between women obtaining an abortion at six to eight weeks and those at 16 to 20 weeks of pregnancy. In addition, these studies have focused on the presence or absence of psychopathological responses to abortion, and not on the emotional aspects of the normative experience in any great detail.[1-9]

It has been our experience that most women respond to abortion with a sense of loss, and that this response is greater in women whose pregnancy has continued into the second trimester. Many authors in the past have described the psychological changes which occur in most women concommitantly with the physiological ones. Deutsch described the process as follows.

The pregnant woman can initially deny the fetus, but once she admits she is pregnant, she feels an unconscious attachment to the fetus. The longer she stays pregnant, the more the fetus becomes a part of her. As a result, after an abortion many women feel that a part of them is gone.[10,11]

In addition to the loss of the fetus, the woman who undergoes an abortion also gives up the role of the pregnant woman. Bibring et al.[12] found that following the abortion the woman has interrupted the developmental processes of pregnancy and terminated the role for which she was physiologically and psychologically preparing.

This chapter focuses upon the experience of abortion in a group of normal women, who, the authors believed, would be at greater risk for responding to abortion with loss and mourning in that they had continued the pregnancy for 16 to 20 weeks. The authors were interested to discover what factors might differentiate between women who would experience loss and mourning in this situation and which might not. A structured interview was devised and a questionnaire designed to detect the presence or absence of loss and mourning. The results of this study have not been reported elsewhere.

Subjects for the study were 30 women who had undergone an amniocentesis abortion at a small private community hospital in California. The criteria for selection were that the women be (1) at least 16 weeks pregnant, (2) receiving an abortion via amniocentesis infusion, (3) English speaking, and (4) not currently under treatment for any emotional disorder.

The women were selected when their abortion was completed. After determining that they met the selection criteria, they were approached in their room. If a patient in any way seemed reluctant to participate or appeared to be sedated or ill, she was thanked for her cooperation and the contact was terminated. The interview was conducted in private, with the patient in bed between one and four hours following the abortion. Each interview lasted about 30 minutes.

Following the interview, each patient was asked to fill out a questionnaire designed to elicit information about perceptions, affects, attitudes, and behaviors related to loss and mourning. The interview had been conducted first in order to reduce any effect that the questionnaire might have on the spontaneity and objectivity of the patient's response to the interview. It consisted of three sections. The first section focused on the demographic data, some of which had been obtained from the chart. The second section consisted of eight questions, each designed to probe for loss-related symptoms. Section three of the interview contained eight sets of affective nonverbal behavioral observations. The questionnaire contained eight sets of questions relating to loss and mourning as perceived by the patient. From the four alternative choices offered for each question, the patient chose the behavior which she felt was most representative for her.

Ages of the patients ranged from 14 to 37, with a mean age of 20.5. The marital status was predominantly single (60 percent). The number of children ranged from zero to eight, with an average of one. One patient had four children, one had eight, 15 had none. Eighteen of the patients were Protestant, nine were Roman Catholic, and three were Latter Day Saints (Mormon). Fifty percent of the patients stated that the church they attended had a negative view on abortion. Forty-six percent stated that they were unaware of their church's view. Thirteen percent of the patients had "positive" views on abortion, 40 percent were "neutral," and 17 percent regarded themselves as "negative" about abortion. Frequency of church attendance ranged from weekly to less than three times a year. Fifty-four percent of the patients attended church weekly or twice monthly.

The reason for seeking an abortion was predominantly one of financial necessity (47 percent). Closely following was not being married or having no male support (40 percent). The rest of the patients obtained the abortion because they were students and wanted to finish school. One subject was raped, but interestingly did not offer this as her reason for seeking abortion.

The results of the data analysis showed that virtually all of the women responded to the abortion with some experience of loss. While most of the loss scores clustered around the mean, it is noteworthy that a few patients exhibited all of the behaviors which were indicative of loss and mourning. This strongly suggests that their experience created a highly significant sense of loss.

Upon totaling the loss scores obtained from each section of the testing instruments, it was found that the observation section of the interview produced the highest loss scores, while the question section of the interview produced the lowest loss scores. From these data it may be inferred that the observation section was more sensitive to loss. Some of the questions in each testing section also appeared to be more sensitive than others.

The demographic data collected showed some relationship to the loss experienced. It would appear that the number of children in the family influenced the patient's reaction to the abortion, i.e., the more children the greater the experience of loss. The older age group seemed to experience a greater degree of loss, while a relatively milder degree of loss was exhibited by the younger group. These findings are in marked contrast to the widely held belief among physicians that an older woman with living children represents a lower risk, from an emotional standpoint, than a younger woman with no living children.

During the course of the interview, the patients made many statements concerning their experiences which were not included in the format of the interview. These expressions substantiated the data obtained from the testing instruments. Direct expression of loss were expressed: "I'm feeling a little empty now," "I feel I've lost something," and "I've nothing to show for all the pain." Women also viewed this experience in future terms: "I don't think I want children now," "It will be with me forever," and "I want to block it out forever." These statements are reflective of similar kinds of grief reactions to death.

We found it noteworthy that all of the patients who were requested to participate in the study agreed without hesitation and completed the interview without exception. They were, for the most part, extremely verbal and responsive. In fact, the only difficulty experienced by the investigators was in focusing the interview on the testing instruments, because the majority of the patients seemed to want to supply more data about their experiences than that which was being solicited. No patients demonstrated any violent or extreme emotional reaction to the questions posed in the testing instruments. A few cried and seemed to find this expression relieving. The women had no difficulty understanding the questions during the interview or in completing the questionnaire.

Women obtaining abortion within the second trimester have waited a significant period of time before deciding and taking action on the termination of pregnancy. This delay may indicate an ambivalence toward the decision of abortion. There may be a relationship between this ambivalence and the experience of loss and post-abortion mourning or even depression. The amniocentesis experience also resembles the labor experience in that the woman is awake and experiences some pain or discomfort when the fetus is delivered. This may be more psychologically significant in relationship to the experiencing of a sense of loss. Most women also view the fetus when it is delivered, an experience different from first trimester abortion.

Although it is likely that some loss and mourning is experienced at whatever stage the pregnancy is terminated, a similar study of first trimester abortions is definitely needed for control.

The absence of the experience of loss in some of the women is also very interesting. These women, usually younger and childless, may not have had the prior personal life experiences which would permit them to experience the abortion as a significant loss.[13]

In summary, the purpose of the study was to evaluate the experience of loss and mourning among a random sample of thirty women undergoing a second trimester therapeutic amniocentesis abortion using a specially constructed interview and questionnaire. The results of the data gathered were analyzed through the use of nonparametric statistics. High scores were indicative of loss and mourning. Significant correlations supported the following conclusions.

1. Marital status: Those who were not married had the lowest scores. Conversely, all of the married patients had high scores (significant to the .05 level).
2. Age and number of children: The correlational matrix revealed that increasing age and number of children was correlated with high scores.
3. Patient's attitude towards abortion: All of the women who expressed negative views towards abortion experienced high scores, while only one patient with a positive view had a high score.
4. Church attendance: The more frequent churchgoers showed higher scores. The opposite was true for those who attended church three times a year or less.
5. Religious preference or the church's attitude towards abortion: These factors did not seem to have any relationship to loss or mourning.
6. The testing instrument was demonstrated to be reliable as indicated by the strength of the relationship of loss scores between the three sections of the testing instrument.

Further analysis of the data supported the thesis that loss was experienced. All patients demonstrated some behaviors indicative of loss. More than one-third of the patients' scores were in the upper quartile of the total range of loss scores. Only three obtained total scores which would not be consistent with the experience of loss. There was a wide range of reactions to the experience of abortion, with a large number of women demonstrating strong loss and mourning responses.

Despite the widely held belief to the contrary among physicians, it appears that increased age and number of children in the family may be used as predictors of mourning following an amniocentesis abortion. It is important that we pay particular attention to this group of women in this day of abortion on demand, and that we help facilitate the mourning process as a normal response to the loss experienced in many of these patients.

REFERENCES

1. Pasnau R: Psychiatric complications of therapeutic abortion. Obstet Gynecol 40:252–256, 1972
2. Kummer J: Post abortion psychiatric illness—a myth? Am J Psychiatry 119:980–983, 1963
3. Simon N, Senturia A: Psychiatric sequellae of abortion: review of the literature 1935–64. Arch Gen Psychiatry 15:378–389, 1966
4. Peck A, Marcus H: Psychiatric sequellae of therapeutic interruption of pregnancy. J Nerv Ment Dis 143:417–425, 1966
5. Simon N, Senturia A, Rothman D: Psychiatric illness following therapeutic abortion. Am J Psychiatry 124:59–65, 1967
6. Patt S, Rappaport R, Banglow P: Follow-up of therapeutic abortion. Arch Gen Psychiatry 20:408–414, 1969
7. Pfeiffer E: Psychiatric indications or psychiatric justifications of the therapeutic abortion. Arch Gen Psychiatry 23:402–407, 1970
8. Ewing J, Rouse B: Therapeutic abortion and a prior psychiatric history. Am J Psychiatry 130:37–40, 1973
9. Proc 81st Ann Conv Psychol Assoc (Montreal, Canada). 8:359–360, 1973
10. Duetsch H: Absence of grief. Psychoanal Q 6:12–22, 1937
11. Duetsch H: Psychology of Women. New York, Grune & Stratton, 1945, Vol 2, pp 126–201
12. Bibring G, Dwyer T, Huntington D, Walenstein A: A study of the psychological processes in pregnancy and of the earliest mother–child relationship. Psychoanal Stud Child 16:9–72, 1961
13. Glasser M, Pasnau R: The unwanted pregnancy in adolescence. J Fam Prac 2:91–94, 1975

Charles E. Hollingsworth
and Robert O. Pasnau

18

Mourning Following
the Birth of a
Handicapped Child

Parents respond to the birth of a physically handicapped or mentally retarded child with many different defenses—denial, guilt, projection, anger, and shame. Grief and mourning reactions are universally
present in these families.

The physical or mental defect is seen as a threat to the parents,
who view the child as an extension of themselves, a way of transcending both and living on. When the defect or retardation is obvious at
birth, the parents feel that they have lost the hope and expectation of
having a normal child. This is a very painful and grief-laden experience. There is little time available for properly mourning the loss because the handicapped child is still there needing special care and
understanding.[1]

Parental defenses are normal. All parents need others to help them
understand and accept even the healthy, nonhandicapped child. It is
not pathological that all parents deny and/or intellectualize to ward off
severe anxiety. However, in the case of parents who have a handicapped child, if their defenses become fixed or unresolved they will
interfere with the parent–child relationship and family dynamics, and
will seriously threaten the emotional health of both parent and child.

Counseling and therapy with a well-trained professional is very important in such cases.

When parents use denial, they may say there is nothing really wrong or the child will outgrow it. They may project the blame by saying it was the fault of the doctor who delivered the baby. They may blame the spouse by saying there are handicapped or mentally retarded relatives in the spouse's family. One or both parents may express guilt, desperately trying to find the cause of the defect. Was it due to smoking or some drug taken during pregnancy? Could it have been prevented? When parents are told by health professionals that the cause of the defect or retardation is unknown, it brings about a revival of each of these fantasies. The hope must be related to reality and tempered by fact.

The other defense is to over-protect the child or become overly involved with the child, ignoring other interests or duties. A healthy balance must be reached between the amount of attention and extra care the child actually needs and the amount given. It is difficult for any parent not to over-protect and allow and encourage the child to develop to his full potential.

Defenses become a problem when they impede the child's development to his full potential or when they adversely affect the family. There are ambivalent feelings toward the handicapped child. Some parents defend by sublimation by becoming very involved in charitable organizations often related to their child's handicap.

If the child appears normal at birth, and the defect or retardation becomes apparent later, usually at age $1^1/_2$ or two years, there is a more gradual adjustment period for the parents to work through their feelings, usually with the help of professional counseling. This gives the child time to become more accepted by the family and to make his place in the family structure.

It is difficult for the physician, or other health professionals who evaluate physically and mentally handicapped children, to answer many of the questions parents ask. It is important that one have adequate training before giving advice based on too little evidence and no hard facts to back up the speculation, predictions, and prognoses. It is just as important not to give false hopes as it is not to give an excessively gloomy outlook. The physician should be a good listener, in touch with the parents' feelings. He should help parents deal with the diagnosis, its label, stigma, pejorative implications, their feelings about the physical handicap or the mental retardation, and, most important, for the future. The goal is one of helping them to acquire understanding, insight, and adjustments in the family dynamics to accommodate for the child's handicap.

There are two important crises for parents of a mentally retarded child. One is the child's entrance into school, known as "going public." The other crisis occurs in adolescence, when the retarded child begins to develop sexually. Parents often need intensive counseling during these crises. Another crisis is centered around the issue of placement of the handicapped or retarded child. Should a child be placed? Why? When? Here, the best guidelines is to consider what is in the best interests of the child. Parents are often afraid that others may feel that they are inadequate or neglecting their duties if they suggest placement. Again, the need for counseling is apparent when this issue is considered.

Chronic mourning is a meaningful way of describing the daily reminder to these parents that they have a handicapped or retarded child. Children with physical handicaps can often learn ways to compensate for their handicap, but unfortunately the mentally retarded children cannot compensate for their loss, and may require more careful supervision and care.

Most parents of physically handicapped or mentally retarded children suffer from chronic sorrow, a pervasive psychological reaction, throughout their lives, regardless of home care or placement.[1] The intensity of the sorrow varies from family to family and from individual to individual. Some parents are more capable of concealing this chronic sorrow from the public than others. The chronic sorrow is usually more intense in the moderate-to-severe handicapped or retarded child's parents than in the groups classed as mildly affected. This chronic sorrow is a natural and understandable response to a tragic fact. The parent can still derive much satisfaction from his handicapped or retarded child's modest achievements in growth and development. Some parents may be too optimistic about a child's potentialities, but it is important to remember that the handicapped child also responds to encouragement, praise, and positive reenforcement. Excessive optimism helps some parents cope with the reality of the child's limitations, which are a daily reminder of the child's handicap.

Some parents do not accept the fact that they have a handicapped or mentally retarded child until the child enters school. Parents of these children are often very concerned about the chances for this child to become a self-sufficient adult. They often worry about who will care for the child if they should die. This may be a realistic concern for some parents, but for others it may be associated with death wishes, either for himself or for his child, which may bring on feelings of guilt which can be associated with depression. The parents' chronic sorrow is produced by the child's dependence, relative changelessness, the unaesthetic quality of defectiveness, and the deep symbolism buried in the process of giving birth to a defective child. The physician should encourage the parents to discuss their feelings of chronic sorrow openly and freely. Such a parent will need time to organize his resources, both internal and external, and to adjust his feelings, so that he can meet the child's needs.

It is very common for parents to seek second and third opinions and evaluations after being told that their child is handicapped or retarded. Some parents continue "doctor shopping" in hopes of finding a cure—magical, scientific, or faddish. Attention should be directed to what answers the parents are searching for, what they fear, what they are denying, and what answers they will accept. Doctor shopping is not necessarily ill-advised—parents are sometimes misinformed by health professionals, or will believe misinformation given to them by well-meaning laymen. Parents sometimes have good reasons to request a second evaluation if they were unsatisfied with a previous evaluation.

The family needs one primary person who can relate information back to them. This person can be the child and family advocate as well as counselor. The communication of facts to the family is only one part of the counseling process and is not necessarily the most important part. It may take several months of counseling to help some parents maintain the strength needed to live with the mentally defective or handicapped child with his limitations. A counselor should not have the goal of doing a one-to-four-hour evaluation with only one feedback session. Most families require at least three to four feedback sessions to allow them time to think of questions, concerns, and issues which they may realize or remember only after the initial feedback information is given. The counselor should repeat the findings, information, conclusions, and prognosis and have family members then repeat what they understand him to have said and what it means to them. The parents need an opportunity to ventilate and clarify their feelings and receive support for the feelings they are expressing. It may be necessary, and is important to work on these same feelings at various times later in the parents' life through follow-up counseling or ongoing therapy. The counselor or therapist assigned to or selected by such a family should be available to them over a very long period of time. The need for repeated and follow-up counseling is not a sign of regression or neurosis. The therapist should be easily accessible to the parents, family and affected child for a recurring problem, a new problem, a crisis, or for difficulty coping with one's feelings. The goal in counseling the parent should be to make the parent more comfortable in living with, managing, and understanding his defective child. Feeding, disciplining, and toilet training the handicapped or retarded child require special considerations, patience, and tolerance of the child's limitations.

Follow-up should be done on every handicapped or retarded child at regular intervals of every three to six months. Parents need to be informed of all available support systems, such as parents' organizations, relatives, ministers, charitable organizations, Red Cross, preschool nurseries, special education classes, day-care centers, and sheltered workshops. Families and parents should be given an opportunity to be away from the child at regular intervals. These respites are valuable for the child and his family! A handicapped or retarded child will necessitate that the babysitter be carefully screened and well trained to care for and supervise the child. The parents will become more accessible to psychological help as they begin to trust the therapist.

The therapist should help the parents make a plan for the immediate future as well as some long range goals. Parents can often benefit from being given some reading materials after the first feedback session after the evaluation is completed. Some excellent references for counselors are listed as references 2–6.

REFERENCES

1. Olshansky S: Chronic sorrow: a response to having a mentally defective child. *In* Robert LN (ed): Counseling Parents of the Mentally Retarded. Springfield, Ill., Charles C. Thomas 1970, pp 49–54
2. Wolfensberger W, Kurtz RA: Management of the Family of the Mentally Retarded Follett Educ. Corp., 1969, 542 p
3. Matheny AP Jr, Vernick J: Parents of the mentally retarded child: emotionally overwhelmed or informationally deprived? Pediatr 74:953–959, 1969
4. Miller L: Toward a greater understanding of the parents of the mentally retarded child. Pediatr 73:699–705, 1968
5. Ryckman B, Henderson A: The meaning of a retarded child for his parents: a focus for counselors. Ment Retard 3(4):4–7, 1965
6. Stevenson A, Heber R: Mental Retardation, Chicago, Ill., University of Chicago Press, 1964

Charles E. Hollingsworth
and Robert O. Pasnau

19

Delayed Grief and
Pathological Mourning

The death of a beloved person normally produces a reactive expression of feeling. The omission of these responses is as much a variation from the normal as are excessively prolonged or intense reactions. Deutsch found that unmanifested grief often is expressed fully in some other way.[1] Psychoanalytic findings also show that guilt feelings toward the lost person, as well as ambivalence, may disturb the normal course of mourning, resulting in a state of severe anxiety. This process may replace the normal process of mourning.

It has been observed that children often do not display any signs of grief or sadness after a death in the family. For many years it was believed that children did not have the intellectual ability to grasp the reality of death, and that there was no grief because of an inadequate formation of object relationships to allow the child to be aware of the loss. Current explanations tend to discard this theory. Child psychiatrists now believe that the personality of the child is not sufficiently developed to bear the strain of the work of mourning. Therefore, the child's ego utilizes narcissistic mechanisms of self-protection to circumvent the mourning process, either by infantile regression expressed as anxiety or by the mobilization of defense forces intended to protect the ego from anxiety and other psychic dangers.[1] Loss may be handled in all the ways listed in Figure 19-1.

It is useful to review briefly these mechanisms of defense, which are used by children and adults to ward off anxiety. It must be stressed that these are unconscious mechanisms of the personality of which the individual who employs them is usually totally unaware.[2] They are

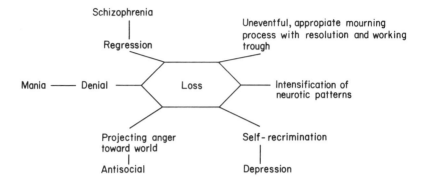

Figure 19-1. Some common psychological reactions to loss.

1. *Denial* of reality: protecting oneself from unpleasant reality by refusal to perceive or face it, sometimes by escaping into physical "illness"
2. *Fantasy:* gratifying frustrated desires in imaginary achievements
3. *Rationalization:* attempting to prove that one's behavior is "rational" and justifiable, and thus worthy of self and social approval
4. *Projection:* placing blame for difficulties upon others or attributing one's own desires to others
5. *Repression:* preventing painful or dangerous thoughts or feelings from entering consciousness
6. *Reaction formation:* preventing dangerous desires from being expressed by exaggerating opposed attitudes and types of behavior and using them as "barriers"
7. *Undoing:* atoning for and thus counteracting unconscious desires or acts
8. *Regression:* retreating to an earlier developmental level involving less mature responses and usually a lower level of functioning
9. *Identification:* avoiding feelings of loss and increasing feelings of worth by becoming like the lost or dead person
10. *Introjection:* incorporating the external values and standards into the personality structure so that the individual is not at their mercy as external threats
11. *Compensation:* covering up weaknesses by emphasizing desirable traits or making up for frustration in one area by overgratification in another

12. *Displacement:* discharging pent-up feelings, usually of hostility or fear, on objects or persons less dangerous than those which initially aroused the emotions

13. *Emotional insulation:* reducing personal involvement and withdrawing into passivity to protect self from hurt

14. *Intellectualization:* cutting off emotional awareness of hurtful situations and separating incompatible attitudes by logic-tight compartments

15. *Sympathism:* striving to gain sympathy from others, thus bolstering feelings of self-worth despite failures

16. *Acting-out:* reducing the anxiety aroused by the loss by permitting their expression in the form of behavior, often of an antisocial or self-destructive nature

17. *Sublimation:* gratifying pent-up feelings, often sexual, in nonsexual productive activities.

Deutsch described a case in which a 30-year-old man was incapable of any emotion whatsoever after learning of his mother's death. He forced himself to recall the most treasured memories of his mother, of her goodness and devotion, but was quite unable to provoke the suffering which he wanted to feel. Subsequently, he could not free himself from the tormenting self-reproach of not having mourned, and he often reviewed the memory of his beloved mother in the hope that he might weep. In his childhood, there had been a period of intensive hatred for the mother which was revived at puberty. Yet as a young man he was closely identified with his mother's passive attitudes and there was a conscious and excessive affection for her. Her death mobilized an infantile reaction in him, ''She has left me,'' with all its accompanying anger. The hate impulses which had arisen in a similar situation of disappointment in his childhood were revived, and, instead of an inner awareness of grief, there resulted a feeling of coldness and indifference due to the interference of the aggressive feelings.[1]

In another case, Deutsch described a 30-year-old man who had no love relationships and who showed the same dull apathetic reaction to all kinds of experiences. He felt that he had ''extraordinary control,'' and saw nothing unusual about his lack of affective response. There was no reaction of grief at the loss of individuals near to him, no unfriendly feelings, and no aggressive impulses. It was learned that this man's mother had died when he was five years old. He had reacted to her death without any feelings. In his later life he had repressed not only the memory of his mother, but also of everything else preceding her death. In the psychoanalytic treatment which followed, only negative and aggressive attitudes towards his mother were revealed. These were related to his resentment of the birth of a younger brother. The only reaction for his dead mother was found in a fantasy, which persisted through several years of his childhood. In the fantasy, he left his bedroom door open in the hope that a large dog would come to him, be very kind to him, and fulfill all his wishes. Apart from this, there was no trace of longing or mourning for his mother.[1]

In these cases we can see many of the mechanisms of defense commonly utilized in cases which we have encountered in our clinical practice as well. After the lengthy illness of a loved one, some people are not emotionally capable of adequately dealing with the impact of death because all their strength had been mustered to help keep the person alive. They may deny the actual death for some time and then begin to deal appropriately with the situation in future weeks or months. If one family member has unresolved grief, other members may try to protect him by not talking about the dead person. This further delays the mourning process.

The syndrome of acute grief may be delayed and may not be dealt with until precipitated by a crisis or an anniversary reaction. Then the grief reaction may be exaggerated. There are many forms of delayed grief reaction. Some survivors experience morbid anxiety attacks with hyperventilitation, choking, weakness, and morbid tension or mental pain if they acknowledge the death of their loved one, so there is a tendency to avoid any and all situations which would require the person to publicly acknowledge the loss. The survivor may refuse visits, become withdrawn, or, on the other hand, may become hypomanic, work long hours, travel extensively, or keep constantly busy with social affairs in order to deliberately keep from thought all references to the deceased.

It is not uncommon for many families to attempt to delay or postpone mourning. If the bereavement occurs at a time when the person is confronted with important tasks and when there is necessity for maintaining the morale of others, he may show little or no reaction for weeks or longer. This delay may involve years, and the person may not be able to express feelings about the more recent death except as it relates to a death which he experienced during the formidable years of childhood. A former unresolved grief reaction may be precipitated in the course of therapy for a delayed reaction to a more recent death.

The precipitating factor for the delayed reaction may be a deliberate recall of circumstances surrounding the death or may be a spontaneous occurrence in the person's life. A peculiar form of this is the circumstance that a person develops the grief reaction at the same time that he himself is as old as the person who died. The delayed reaction may occur after an interval which is not marked by any abnormal behavior or distress, but in which there has developed an alteration in the person's conduct which is the surface manifestation of an unresolved grief reaction.

In our modern times, some dying pesons, in their effort to spare the survivors the pain of mourning, request that the family not be sad, that they hold no funeral services, and they they have a joyous party after the death. This only postpones the resolution of deep emotions which are more appropriately handled by direct confrontation immediately after the death by facing the realistic facts and circumstances. Pretending that the death has not occurred and that the entire family is happy is neither realistic, honest, nor healthy.

Lindeman classified pathological forms of mourning as follows:

1. Overactivity without a sense of loss, rather with a sense of well-being and zest, the activities being of an expansive and adventurous nature and bearing semblance to the activities formerly carried out by the deceased
2. The acquisition of symptoms belonging to the illness of the deceased
3. Exacerbations of psychosomatic conditions, such as ulcerative colitis, asthma, and rheumatoid arthritis
4. Alterations in relationship to friends and relatives, with the likelihood that the bereaved person will become withdrawn and will need considerable encouragement in re-establishing his social relationships
5. Furious hostility against specific persons, usually the physicians and caretakers of the deceased, or family and friends who did not visit during the deceased loved one's illness
6. Decompensation into a psychotic depression with tension, agitation, insomnia, feelings of worthlessness, bitter self-accustation, and obvious need for punishment. Such individuals may be dangerously suicidal[3]

The bereaved may be excessively preoccupied with feelings of guilt. He may search the time before the death for evidence of failure to do right by the lost one. He accuses himself of negligence and exaggerates minor omissions.

According to Hackett, normal grief lasts from four to 12 weeks, with a spectrum of three stages: (1) Denial of loss, in which the bereaved may have vivid dreams of the deceased, or imagine seeing him in a crowd; (2) full acceptance, accompanied by depression and despair; and (3) reorganization, during which time the bereaved makes adjustments in his or her life to carry forth without the deceased. By contrast, he described six important distress signs for persons with pathological mourning. These are: (1) Unduly prolonged grieving; (2) false euphoria; (3) self-destructive impulses; (4) over-reaction to another person's trouble; (5) development of symptoms of the deceased; and (6) unaccountable sadness at a certain time of the year.[4]

Grief may be prolonged for many reasons, not all of which are abnormal. Parents who have become very attached to a young child may grieve for months if the child dies. An elderly person whose spouse of many years dies may also have prolonged grief. Persons with previous depressions may mourn for longer-than-usual periods. In patients with a history of cyclical mood swings a false euphoria in response to a death may be observed. Friends may feel that this sense of well-being and elation is inappropriate. When the denial of the loss ends, so does the euphoria. At such time, the bereaved may plunge into a deep depression. A person with a severe obsessive personality disorder also may develop an agitated depression after a loved one dies.

Physicians and health care workers should be alert for hazards of abnormal grieving. Some people who suffer from abnormal grief are reacting as if a part of them had died or as an overreaction to the life style that they have been denied because of the death of their partner. Some people turn to alcohol during prolonged grief, but in most cases the alcoholism was a problem before the death, and the alcoholism is blamed on the tragic death.

Physicians and health professionals should be especially alert for the bereaved person who invests unwisely, gambles recklessly, turns away from old friends, takes up high risk activities such as auto racing or skydiving, or engages in other potentially self-destructive behavior following the loss of a significant loved one. The person engaging in such behavior is unaware that he may be driven by unconscious guilt or anxiety over the person who died.

During prolonged grief reactions a person may cry excessively at the most unpredictable moment and over the most trivial incident. He may have an exaggerated response to some other person's trouble or misfortune which may trigger his own submerged feelings of loss and self-recrimination. The painful emotional ordeal could have been briefer and easier if the person had been encouraged to grieve at the appropriate time. In addition, he may develop symptoms or problems of the deceased. One example is a person who develops alcoholism following the death of a mother, father, or spouse from alcoholic cirrhosis.

In a family which does not permit the expression of emotion, we often see a delayed grief reaction. Friends who praise a widow or the parents of a dead child for remaining composed through funeral rituals are not helping the bereaved. Unexpressed grief always has a detrimental effect on one's mental health. It may manifest as malaise, lethargy, insomnia, or decreased interest in sexual activity.

In the case of a prolonged terminal illness, the family may have entered the mourning process long before death occurs by recognizing the realistic situation and using anticipatory grief. However, even in such cases, some post-death grief and mourning should be expected.

The Davidson family presents examples of a delayed grief and pathological mourning in a family. The father died at age 34 after being ill for one year. This reaction was marked by anxiety and depression in the mother and separation anxiety in one of the children. Mrs. Davidson sought professional help for herself and her eldest son Jason, age 10, eight months after her husband's death and four months after she and her two sons finally began the painful mourning process. The delayed reaction was partially a consequence of the deceased husband's request that the family not mourn, but be joyous and jovial after his death. They complied by having no funeral and giving a party the day after he died. In addition, the mother found it impossible to express grief and loss in the presence of her own mother, who came to live with her for three months after her husband died. After Grandmother left, the children noted that their mother began to cry, seemed depressed, and talked much more about their deceased father. At that time they were also able to begin realistically mourning the death of their father. Unfortunately, by that time Jason was having difficulties in separating from his mother, and teachers had noted that he became very anxious and worried about his mother while at school. After only 12 visits with a psychotherapist, both the mother and the oldest son were able to proceed with the mourning process. The boy was no longer having separation problems from his mother. He was able to stay in school without being anxious about his mother. The mother was referred for weekly group therapy for the next few months, where she had a further opportunity to explore her feelings.

The therapeutic interaction which follows is distilled from several tape-recorded interviews. It provides many examples of problems seen in a family in mourning, especially in a modern family that tries to live by an idealistic philosophy which encourages denial of the sadness of the loss of a loved one. This dialogue also illustrates some of the stress on the family of the terminal patient and the children's response to their father's death, which is typical of the response of many families. All the names have been changed. (In the transcript which follows, J = Jason, M = Mother, P = psychotherapist.)

J: My father's death is a very private thing.

M: Jason is very private with his feelings. I don't think he really understands what is going to be accomplished from us getting together. He is probably going to ask me the same things that he asked last week after we left, since he doesn't really understand the concepts we are dealing with. But I told him that it is good that we can talk about our feelings and air them and get them out in the open, rather than holding them in. Maybe there are a lot of things that bother him that he doesn't even know about. I noticed he was apprehensive on the way over today, so I'm sure he has anxiety about our meeting.

P: Jason, we are concerned about what you are feeling and what you have been worrying about.

M: Last weekend I went away for the weekend and left my children with a girlfriend and Jason seemed to adjust well to that. It was the first time I have been away from my children overnight in six years.

J: As long as I'm staying with someone, and not bored, I don't mind. Sometimes I'm bored at home. I can think of things to do on weekdays while I'm at school, but then on the weekends I really miss my dad, and I can't remember the things I wanted to do; or if I try them, sometimes I can't do it.

P: I would like for us to spend some time today talking about the death of your father and the request that he made before he died—that you be happy after he died and have a party rather than a sad funeral. It seems that you and your mother waited a long time before you allowed yourself to begin mourning.

J: There is one thing my father always said. "Every day can be a holiday. You can have parties any time you want. You don't have to wait until holidays to have parties; you can do it any day," and I believe in that very strongly. Mom, didn't someone say that Dad was quite a philosopher?

M: I don't remember who said it, but he was quite an individual, wasn't he? He certainly thought for himself, didn't he?

P: Do you think, perhaps, both of you wanted to show the other how strong you could be after your dad died?

J: Yes, I think so. We're doing pretty good now, aren't we, Mom? For my mom it was harder about four months after my dad died. Right after he died, most of the time my mother would stop thinking about it, she was so busy. Maybe she would stop sometime and think about it, but we were so busy during that time. We would go on trips and, like, maybe a couple of months ago my mom started to cry, and it would upset me so when she started to cry.

P: Did you cry about it yourself when she would cry?

J: No, I didn't cry about it myself, but I felt sad. It seems that when you are young you don't cry as much about it, but when you are older you just cry a lot more.

P: Were you ever afraid to let your mother see how sad you were?

J: No, but if I cried, I felt kind of embarrassed in front of everyone, so I just kept the sadness in my mind. I just wanted to show my Mom that I was strong so she could hold together better.

P: Mrs. Davidson, did you feel that you had to hold together and not cry in the presence of the boys?

M: No, I didn't feel that way at all. I felt that I would just do what came natural for me and when it came out, it came out natural. Both of my sons usually comforted me when I cried, especially Jason. I remember one time at night I was crying alone in my room and Jason came and he wrapped himself around me, and Jeff came and he wrapped himself around me. They were like two snakes wrapped around me, loving me and petting me. When Jason is around when I cry, he comes and holds me, comforts me, and shares it with me. I don't know if it worries him, or whether it gets it out of his system at all, but I felt that I certainly wanted them to see me cry. I never wanted to hide it from anyone, except my mother, who stayed with us for a while after my husband died. After she left, I just felt that I could let down my defenses and really begin to cry. I have encouraged the boys to get their feelings out. When I told the boys their father had died . . .

J: I didn't even know he had died.

M: Well, you were sleeping, and, darling, that is why I didn't want to wake you up.

J: I woke up and I went downstairs to say good morning to him and . . .

M: You came in to see me first, and [turning to therapist] I told him to think about the worst thing that could happen, but he didn't think about that, and then I told him his father had died. And he really understood it. He was so grown up about it. He asked me what happened to him, where his body was, and when he would be buried. They were practical kinds of things; well, that's just the way it was. And he spent some time talking to me about it afterwards; then Jason told his brother; I had wanted to tell him, but I had to go across the street, and when I came back Jason had told him, and when I came back I wanted to talk to the other child about it, but he didn't want to talk about it. He just went back and got in his bed and then in about two hours he just went berserk, running around the house, pulling all the bed covers off, turning over chairs, just upsetting everything, but he didn't break anything.

J: Why did he do that?

M: 'Cause he was upset, and that is how he was relieving his anger.

J: Upset about what?

M: Because Daddy died.

J: He wasn't upset. He didn't do any of that.

M: But he did do it, you saw him doing it. He went running around the house . . .

J: He wouldn't do that.

M: Maybe you didn't see him, but he ran around . . .

P: I think one thing we should look at, Jason, is your reaction when you said she didn't come wake you up when he died, and what your feelings are in regards to not finding out until the next morning.

J: I don't know. I just thought that he was still alive. Dead?

P: Do you feel that she should have come and woke you up when he died?

J: No, maybe I would have been more upset then.

P: Do you think she wanted to take care of arrangements before she told you?

J: Probably.

P: Does that make it difficult to trust your mother?

J: What do you mean?

P: It seems you worry a lot about her, and I was wondering if you have difficulty trusting her.

J: I can trust her a lot. Nothing has been happening to her.

P: Do you think she will tell you everything you need to know?

J: Yes, if I really needed to know, she would probably explain things to me.

P: What kind of things do you think she might keep secret from you?

J: Just things that might upset me. She doesn't really have any secrets from me, but I know . . .

P: Do you think you have gone through several months of mourning since your father died?

J: I've tried to keep it off my mind, so I won't be sad, but it is good to think about it once in a while.

M: There even got to be a point last summer, after a month or two, when I had to say, "Do you even remember your father?" They just seemed so normal. It was as if they never had a father. I was wondering what is going on in their minds. Somehow they were capable of just accepting it and pushing it completely out of their minds. I mean, they didn't even make reference to him. Sometimes they would look at pictures of him. I finally said, "Don't you guys even think about your father? Do you even remember what he looked like?" They said they think about him once in a while, so I thought maybe that is just the way it is with kids. I was 17 when my father died. I guess it was very different for me than for them.

P: Jason, do you ever feel nervous at school?

J: Worried, you mean? Yes, sometimes I used to, but then I told my teacher about it, and then she says teachers are not only for teaching, they are also for helping, so now I know that she would help me if I do get worried.

P: What kind of things would you get worried about?

J: I can't remember.

P: Could you try to remember?

J: What? It's hard. I've had to tell the teachers sometimes that I'm worried about my mom.

P: I'd like to spend the remainder of today's session with Jason alone. [*Mother leaves the room. Jason cries because she is leaving him.*]

M: Sweetie, what's the matter? I'll just be sitting outside the door, darling.

J: [*Sobbing quietly*]

P: What are you thinking about, Jason?

J: I'm afraid I might get lost in this building.

P: Were you afraid for your Mom to leave just now?

J   Yes, sometimes I'm afraid she might leave and not come back until half an hour later, and I won't be knowing what has happened to her. It happens lots of times at home and at school. I don't mind in school, but sometimes after school, I think she is planning to pick me up, and she doesn't come, and I don't know what has happened.

P: Do you think the fact that your father has died makes you much more worried about your mother coming late or not being there?

J: Yes.

P: Were you ever able to really break down and cry a lot about your father dying?

J: No.

P: Why not?

J: 'Cause I wasn't sad enough; it is hard for me to cry.

P: But it is okay to cry. It is one way to reach your feelings. Did you feel like your mom expected you not to cry?

J: I guess she didn't know if I was going to cry or not.

P: What kind of things have been on your mind that you would like to talk to me about?

J: I don't remember. I have forgotten them all. It is too hard to explain. I'm still thinking about my Mom out there. That is why I'm coming to see you, because I worry about where my mom is too much. I'm afraid I might get lost in this building.

P: Is your teacher like your mom in some ways?

J: Yes. It was okay with me that my mom went out of town.

P: Do you ever worry any about your health?

J: No.

P: Do you ever worry that you might get that same illness your father had?

J: No. I try to be careful. I ride my bicycle and skateboard very carefully. Sometimes I go off by myself to think.

P: Sometimes it is very painful to talk about sad things, but it often helps to share those thoughts with someone, and that is why I will be talking with you each week.

J: Sometimes I'm afraid to ride in elevators. I'm afraid I might get trapped inside. I have a cat that looks like a tiger and two dogs.

P: Who feeds them?

J: Me, my brother, and my mom.

P: Are they well cared for?

J: Yes, and the neighbor's dog had puppies that look like my dog.

P: Did your dog go over and see his puppies?

J: He never really cared about them. I showed them to him, but he didn't seem to care. He's completely different from us. See, they don't need a father any more, just a mother. I mean sometimes the father dog helps protect them.

P: Is that what you miss about your father, him protecting you?

J: No, that's not it. It is just that I miss him.

P: In some ways, maybe you feel that your dad left you, like your pet left his puppies.

J: No, I mean my dog would have stayed with his puppies and teach them how to swim, but with my father it was different. He had no choice. He took me out sometimes, but sometimes he came home late at night. I never thought about my dad dying before he got sick. But I always worry about my mom, or that I might get lost somewhere, and I might end up on another planet somewhere, and my mom would be worried about me. Or that I might be running along and just sink down in a hole. But, I know it is impossible, but I still daydream about it.

P: Do you ever think about wanting to be with your dad?

J: No, he's sort of off my mind, and he's not really with me, so I don't ever think about it. It is so good to think about my father, though. I try to remember the important things about my father like his birthday and the date he died.

After several weeks of joint sessions, Mrs. Davidson was seen alone.

M: They are good children. I really don't have discipline or social problems with either of them. Jason can't stay the night at someone's house, whereas Jeff can.

P: Have you had any problems with neighbors or relatives talking about you?

M: Any gossiping about me? I don't know, maybe they think I am an immoral widow. How about all the gossip I had to endure after my husband died? My brother-in-law took all of his frustrations and anger for the death of his brother out on me, just at the point that my husband was dying and after he had died. He accused me of murdering my husband. He accused me of standing at the door when they took his body out and of laughing and shouting, "You had a good life." He accused me of adultery. On the day my husband died I called him to come over to help me. When he stopped breathing I asked him to see if the heart was beating, I guess, and he said "No." He said, "You call your friends out there." He was standing by the bed and he wouldn't help me change his clothes. And that was the first time my husband was incontinent, in the final hour.

Well, what would you do with a person like my brother-in-law? He is not going to know right from wrong. I'll just avoid him. I'm not a vindictive person.

Afterwards, one of my husband's friends asked, "Please, could the priest just say a prayer over his body?'' And they said please do it for the sake of his parents. And I said okay, let the priest do it. So the priest went to the funeral home; it was really a very charming scene. My mother and three or four of my closest friends were there with me. They had just finished the autopsy and threw a sheet over him and wheeled him by. I could have stayed home, but it didn't seem right. I'm glad I was there. But that brother of his would not go. See, the prayer was done for the family, so he went and told all our friends that I had conspired to keep him from attending his own brother's funeral. Yet he came to my house the day before and said he was going out of town. I think he felt we weren't doing it the right way.

P: Did your sons attend the prayer service?

M: No, I told them when he would be buried, and I just said he would be buried next to my father at the church where the boys were baptized. So that is all I told them; it just didn't seem any point to tell them much else. When I picked up the ashes, my mother said, ''Don't tell the children what you have in the little box.'' I mean, she really didn't have to say anything. Why should they see that little box and ask, is that their father? It might be a very frightening thing for them.

P: I agree, especially at their age.

M: I don't know if it would or wouldn't be; I did tell them that he was cremated, but I don't know if they know the meaning; I don't see any point of explaining until they ask. But I did tell them that he was buried in a coffin. I don't know if I did right or not. I will answer as much as they ask, but I wait until they ask and they ask me a lot. They asked me early about sex, and I explained it all to them, and they seemed to understand, and I showed books to them, but I just went to the level that they wanted. So I thought with this, that that would be just to the level that they would want.

P: That seems to be a very healthy approach to take. It is like the story of the little boy who asked his mother where he came from, and she explained all the details of reproduction, and the boy said, ''Well, Johnny said he came from Trenton, and I just wondered where I was from.'' [*Both laugh.*] But, you seem to be answering *only* the questions they ask.

M: It's not that I try to hide anything from them. When my husband died, Jason asked if he was downstairs and I said no, but he didn't ask exactly where he was taken or anything about the autopsy. Then, four months later, my mother took his ashes home with her and kept them in her closet for another three months. When you think about it, the whole concept of death becomes so incredible. It doesn't make much sense to me.

P: Sometimes it can be very painful to think about it. Especially for us to think about our own death.

M: Death is a very painful subject for me. It has been painful since I can remember, and I used to write a great deal of poetry about death because it plagued me, and I haven't found an answer. I experienced three deaths the year I was 18—my grandmother of a stroke, my boyfriend of a car accident, and my father of an accidental death, all in one year within three months' time. I began to worry that my husband would get killed driving his car, and if he was late coming home I was a nervous wreck. I just thought something might happen to him. When I was 20 I had a legal abortion, and at that time I had no real opinion on the subject, but I later came to view it as putting death to my own creation. I consider it to be murder, really; I just don't know how I did it. It was life, and I took it away. I've never forgiven myself for that. Would I do it again? No.

My husband didn't seem to mind dying. He would never discuss death with me. If I woke up in the middle of the night and wanted to tell him that I was terrified of death, he wouldn't discuss it. He said, "I'll worry about it just before I am dying, but I'm not going to talk about it until then." He was too full of life. He was not a negative thinker; see, I'm much more of a negative thinker.

P: That is probably why positive thinking helped him so much to cope with his own finiteness.

M: When he was near the end, he cried. He didn't want to leave me and the children, and so he cried for that sadness. But as far as dying, he said, "Look, we all have to die. I may be better off than all of you." So I couldn't argue with that.

P: Are there any problems arising in your role change with your sons since your husband's death?

M: I think I feel some conflict in the style of child rearing, but I think my only conflict with them is that I will have to be away from home a lot more than I would like to be, if I have to take a job. But sometimes those adjustments are necessary in life. I think their conduct and my conduct in the home is okay. I plan to take a job, but I haven't really started to look yet. I was too depressed a month ago, but I feel better now. It is up to me to change. I can't change my husband's death. I think I was expecting a delayed reaction, and so I had it.

The case of the Davidson family shows both delayed grief and pathological mourning. Because of respect for her husband's wishes, with which she complied because of her own background and past failure to deal adequately as a teenager with the loss of her father, no formal religious or family ritual was held. Perhaps because the presence of her own mother, whom she was trying to protect, and facing the accusations of her angry brother-in-law, Mrs. Davidson was unable to begin her period of mourning. While her younger son Jeff expressed his feelings with a transient episode of angry destructive behavior, Jason, the ten-year-old with a precocious sense of his own responsibility, tried to be the "man of the house" and the source of strength for his mother, whom he perceived to be at risk. He attempted to deal with his anxiety by phobic displacement, which was symbolically related to his unconscious fears of death (elevators = coffins?) and separation.

This case also points out some techniques of working with such families. In the past, religious agencies have led in dealing with the bereaved. They have provided comfort by giving the backing of dogma to the patient's wish for continued interaction with the deceased, have developed rituals which maintain the patient's interaction with others, and have counteracted the morbid guilt feelings of the patient by Divine Grace and by promising an opportunity for "making up" to the deceased at the time of later reunion.[4] Unfortunately, the Davidsons were denied this support.

While these efforts have helped countless mourners, comfort alone does not provide adequate assistance in the patient's grief work. The mourner's task is to accept the pain of the bereavement and to review his relationship with the deceased. He needs to become acquainted with the alterations in his own modes of emotional reaction, his fear of insanity, and particularly his fear of accepting the surprising changes in his feelings. Finally, he needs to express his sorrow and sense of loss. The psychiatrist or psychotherapist's goal in treating a family with a delayed grief reaction or pathological mourning is to emancipate the survivors from the "bondage of the deceased," to help them readjust to the environment from which the deceased is missing, and to encourage the formation of new relationships with appropriate adjustment in family dynamics.

REFERENCES

1. Duetsch H: Absence of grief. Psychoanal Q 6:12–22, 1937
2. Kolb L: Modern Clinical Psychiatry. Philadelphia, Saunders, 1973, 8th ed., pp 60–86
3. Lindemann E: Symptomatology and management of acute grief. Am J Psychiatry 101:141–148, 1944
4. Hackett TP: Recognizing and treating abnormal grief. Hosp Physician 10:49–56, 1974

PART IV

Helping the Family in Mourning

Charles E. Hollingsworth
and Robert O. Pasnau

20

The Role of Religion
for Bereaved Families

Nature does not know extinction; all it
knows is transformation. Everything
science has taught me, and continues to
teach me, strengthens my belief in the continuity of our spiritual existence after
death.[1]

Wernher von Braun

With the increasing secularization of modern life has come the progressive decline in adherence to formal mourning practices over the past
several decades. This change has apparently deprived many individuals of the support of religious custom in organizing their behavior and
activities during the period of acute grief. The importance of open
expression of grief and of friends, relations, and memories during the
mourning period seem to be unappreciated by large segments of the
population. It is expected that they will resume ordinary activities,
show no public evidence of grief, and carry the burden of the loss
stoically and alone.

For those with religious faith, however, the situation may be different. Traditional expressions of grief and rituals remain an important part of the religious process in many of the major religions. It is important that the physician and other health-care team members become aware of the significance of religious beliefs and traditions which may be different from their own, so that they may help to initiate the involvement of the family with their own religious group or tradition at the time of the death in the family. In this chapter, we will review the beliefs and traditions of some of the important Christian groups, including the major Protestant sects, the Roman Catholics, the Latter Day Saints (Mormons), and the Christian Scientists. We will also look at the traditions and beliefs of Judaism, Islam, Buddhism, and Hinduism.

There are marked differences in the Protestant religious traditions and rituals regarding funerals and mourning. In the fundamentalist groups, such as the Baptists, Pentacostals, and other evangelical sects, the families often have an intense and long-standing involvement in a particular church or religious congregation. Usually the pastor has been involved with the family before the death, and the church group has already moved in to offer support to the family, with help in the arrangements for the funeral and services. Because these groups interpret the Bible in a literal fashion, they believe in the actual physical resurrection of their loved one on the Day of Judgment. Sometimes, autopsy permission is denied because of the fantasy of resurrection with disfigurement, even though the theology of their church is inconsistent with this idea. Nonetheless, grieving is often intense and open, with loud expressions of weeping and even shouting. Families from these sects believe in a literal heaven for those who have been saved through the acceptance of Christ as a "personal savior" by a process known as "vicarious atonement." If one truly believes that Jesus died on the cross to atone for the person's own sins against God and accepts God into his heart, then he is "born again" or saved. On the other hand, if one has not been saved he will surely go to eternal damnation and punishment for his sins. Such beliefs are deeply held and seem to be reassuring to the family members at the time of the death of a loved one, particularly if the deceased has been a good church member and has been "saved." It can work in the reverse for the families of a deceased love one who has given up the belief prior to death or who never was "saved." In such situations it is advised that the physician alert the pastor that the family may need some special help and prayer.

In families who belong to the more liberal Protestant groups (those which have varying nonliteral interpretations of the Bible), including the Methodists, Presbyterians, Congregationalists, and others, often there is found a less involved relationship with their church and their minister. The minister may only come if called upon by the family. The church will provide the necessary facilities for the funeral service, but often the relationship of the members of the congregation with each other is informal. For such families, the physician may need to take a more active role in initiating the contact with the church. Whereas many liberal Protestant families have beliefs similar to those of the fundamentalists, many do not. Death comes with many questions which are difficult for their minister to answer for them. Their belief in heaven may be in a largely symbolic way, that is, that their loved one lives on in the memories of the bereaved family and friends. Almost none of these families believe in the resurrection of the body on the Day of Judgment. If there is a belief in an afterlife, it is assumed that it is achieved at the time of death. In most of the major liberal denominations, the concept of hell has been abandoned or de-emphasized in keeping with a positive approach to life and the Christian philosophy of brotherly love in relationships with fellow men. Funerals and religious rituals are similarly de-emphasized. The proceedings are simple, quiet, dignified. Mourning is also quiet, and grief is not expressed as openly or intensely.

For Roman Catholic families, the situation is quite different. As with the fundamentalist Protestant families, usually they have been deeply involved in a particular parish church, and the priest has visited with the family prior to the death. At the time of the death, there may have been a final confession and absolution of sins, followed by the passage of the immortal soul into limbo. The Roman Catholics believe that the final sacrament of burial will release the soul into heaven. The ritual is well known to all family members and helps to organize their behavior during the acute grief phase. National and cultural differences are important to understand as well. In Italian, Spanish, and Latin American cultures, Roman Catholics wear black to the funeral. There is a trend in America away from this tradition except for the immediate family. After the death, a wake is held for 24 to 48 hours. The body is at the mortuary, and a rosary is usually held on the night before the funeral, with family members going into the slumber room at the mortuary to view the body and say the prayers. The priest comes to the mortuary each night of the wake, usually in the last half hour of the waking ceremony, and family members gather around him to view the body and recite the rosary. The older and more traditional the culture, the longer the wake. The average wake is two days long, with an open casket in the mortuary. A requiem mass is held in the church with a closed casket. The funeral procession is led by the body of the deceased, followed by the immediate family, then friends and acquaintances. At the cemetery, the priest is present and the casket is not lowered into the ground until the immediate family has left. Catholics do not have an elaborate ritual for mourning. Mourning is left up to the individual and close family members, with relatives bringing food and visiting frequently in the early mourning period. Catholics usually have a yearly mass in honor of the deceased on the date of the person's death, usually in the early morning, with the family making a donation to the church. The mass is attended by family members and close friends.

The Latter Day Saints (Mormons) hardly consider death at all. They view death as a temporary separation. Family units go on after death, relationships with other people go on, and if people have not been grossly sinful, then loved ones will be together after death, children will be together with parents, brothers with sisters, and husbands with wives. Families go on just as the would have with everyone together. Death is a brief separation, like taking a trip, not a permanent separation. Since the separation at death is a temporary thing, the funeral is designed to be rather emotionally uplifting. At the funeral, there are two or three brief sermons about the impermanence of death, stressing that death is insignificant, that life goes on forever, that every being has always existed, and, just like God, "there has always been you and me." Death is a passage from one stage to another, and friendships and relationships that are formed in this life will continue through all time and all existence.

After the death, all the family (including the extended family) come together. When possible, the surrounding neighborhood takes in visitors and family who have come to attend the funeral. The gathering may encompass several hundred people. The funeral can be held at any time after the death, with open or closed casket. The funeral service is held in the church or the mortuary. Rarely is the body brought to the home. There is a brief graveside prayer for the dedication of the grave. The tombstone may be put up at any time after the funeral. After the funeral, friends in the neighborhood bring food to the home, and family and friends talk for several hours. On special occasions, family members and/or friends may take flowers to the grave. The predominant feeling is that death really is not important. Mourning for separation is considered acceptable, and the mourning may go on for some time, with sadness about separation. On the other hand, it is stressed that the bereaved will be with the loved one afterwards; he is not lost, he is not gone. Life goes on, and there is no reason to be unhappy.

The physician should be aware that this belief may pose a problem for a family member whose grief is prolonged. He may feel guilty about this and confide to the doctor, "Why don't I believe in my religion enough? My religion tells me that I should not be sad for such a long period." The person should be reassured that the mourning process is largely an unconscious process, and takes longer for some than for others. For some Mormon families, the emphasis on "not being sad" may hinder the normal mourning process. In such cases, the family should be advised to talk about the problem with their bishop.

For Christian Science families, and for members of a sect called Science of Mind, the inevitability of mourning and grieving is not accepted. They believe that one must learn to accept such losses. They teach that Jesus was a positive thinker, and that if a person holds a wish in his mind and believes that he can accomplish the wish, it will be possible. They believe that this type of faith—positive thinking—has healing power. It is made effective by the afflicted person himself. Faith and a positive attitude are important variables in the patient's convalescence or during a prolonged terminal illness. For those families, the problem of the physician is very great. Usually, the members do not consult physicians because of their antipathy towards the medical model of illness. Great tact, skill, and understanding must be employed to help the family accept the loss without threatening the ideal of death without grief. We believe that members of these groups may be at special risk for the development of pathological grief reactions. Nonetheless, their belief must be respected and understood by those who would attempt to help them deal with their loss.

Jewish tradition confronts death directly. In this faith, the period of terminal illness and dying is viewed as a time when loved ones should surround and comfort the terminally ill family member. He is encouraged to put his worldly and spiritual affairs in order. The death-bed confessional prayer is viewed as an important element in the transition to the world to come. This deathbed scene is thus structured to give the dying person an outlet for expression of natural concerns and anxieties. Jews do not believe in a life hereafter. It is believed that it is important to lead a decent, good, helping life on earth.

Many years ago, if no doctor was present to pronounce the person dead, a family member would put a feather at the person's mouth to determine if it moved, or a mirror to see if steam collected on the mirror. If there was no sign, the family kept a close watch over the body until the deceased was taken to the mortuary.

There are considerable differences in the mourning ritual within Judaism, which are determined by the type of faith. In the Orthodox tradition, black is not worn for mourning. All mirrors in the home are covered for one week after a family member has died. Mirrors may be covered with any type of material. This ritual is performed in order to prevent the appearance of evil spirits. The face of the deceased is not covered and the body is not wrapped for the first 24 hours after the death. The loved one must be buried within 24 hours after the death, but not between sundown on Friday and sundown on Saturday, or not until after religious services are over on Saturday. The body is not viewed after death and there is a closed casket at the funeral, which is held at the synagogue. Orthodox Jewish men are buried with a *yarmulke* (cap) and in a prayer shawl called a *tallith*. Many families have the tradition of washing their hands before they enter their home after a funeral. After the funeral, the nuclear family sits *shivah* (Hebrew for seven) for seven days without leaving the house, sitting closely together without wearing shoes or stockings. This period is one of intense mourning with prayers and readings about death. Relatives and close friends bring in food and/or gifts. Each night during the *shivah*, when 10 adult men have gathered in the home, the *minyan* (Hebrew for quorum) of special prayers is said for a public service in the home with family and close friends of the deceased. Many years ago, mourning family members put ashes on their head and wrapped their bodies in a sack during the *shivah*. They do not change their clothes during the seven-day period.

The family does not go to the gravesite for one full year after the burial. Then, on the first anniversary of the burial, the Yahrzeit, close relatives, friends, and the Rabbi go to the gravesite for the unveiling of the tombstone. The Rabbi must be present for the unveiling. Each year, on the anniversary of the death, according to the Jewish calendar, a candle is lit in the home. One candle is lit for each death on that particular date. On Yom Kippur, a day of fasting which occurs eight days after the Jewish New Year, a memorial candle is lit in the home and synagogue for each deceased member of the nuclear family. Candles may also be lit for deceased cousins if no one from their nuclear family is able to represent them. Families who had relatives killed in concentration camps follow the tradition of lighting one candle at Yom Kippur for each immediate family member who died in a concentration camp, or were not heard from after being placed in a concentration camp, and presumed to be dead. It is also possible to make a donation at the synagogue for an electrical candle, which stays lit all year long, named in memory of the deceased family member. This donation is renewed on the anniversary of the death according to the Jewish calendar. For the Orthodox Jews, who by tradition may have a secular, that is, non-Jewish name as well as a Jewish name, the Jewish name is used at the memorial service for lighting candles. These Jewish names for children are selected to honor a deceased family member by naming the new child after someone who has died in the family, such as a grandparent, aunt, uncle, cousin, or sibling. If the family has lost a child and another child is born of the same sex, the new child automatically gets the Jewish name of the deceased child. If the new child is of opposite sex, then the name is selected from some other deceased family member.

Conservative Jews have retained many of the Orthodox traditions. They sometimes beat on their chests, and cry and wail at the gravesite service or during the *shivah* if they feel they have sinned in any way against the deceased member. This practice is also followed on high holidays to ask for forgiveness of sins by Orthodox and Conservative Jews.

Liberal Reform Jews have made many changes in the Orthodox traditions. The ritual for handling death and mourning is an optional matter for the individual, and some traditions are no longer practiced. For Reform Jews, the Yahrzeit is not a time of mourning, but a time of remembrance.

All three traditions of Judaism view the confrontation of death and the reaffirmation of life as dual responsibilities. Jewish tradition contains a positive pattern of observance through which the individual is enabled to confront the crisis of bereavement. All of these traditions emphasize the continuity of life through the family, and close family ties are reaffirmed in the rituals of Jewish mourning. In Judaism all aspects of funeral arrangements, including the selection of a casket, are governed by principles of simplicity and the acceptance of the reality of death.[2]

For families who belong to the Muslim or Islamic faith, the divinely inspired teachings of Muhammad and his apostles have been preserved in a book called the Qurān, which they believe is a faithful and unalterable reproduction of the original scriptures which are preserved in heaven. In sickness, the Qurān is the Muslim families' standby. Friends and relatives will enter the sick-chamber and recite favorite verses. Some people never leave their homes without having a small copy of the Qurān on their person. The bereaved find great consolation in reading it.

Although there are several sects of Islamic tradition, all of the sects believe in Heaven and Hell. The orthodox believe in predestination, with man's fate being fixed before he is born. Other sects believe that man has full responsibility for his acts, but that this responsibility is accompanied by its necessary consequences. If man commits mortal sins, he is condemned to Hell forever, with no prospect of escape.

The Muslim creed, known as Fiqh Akbar II, was compiled about

A.D. 1000. It is based largely on the teachings of Ash'ari, the most prominent figure in the formative period of Islamic theology. It teaches that Allah is absolute in his decrees of good and evil. He does not resemble his creatures in any respect. He has existed from eternity with his qualities, those belonging to his essence and those pertaining to his activity. The Qurān is the speech of Allah written in books, preserved in memories, recited by tongues, revealed to the prophet. The doctrine of predestination is tempered, according to the Qurān, by saying that its writing is of a descriptive, not a deceptive, nature. God may punish a sinner by sending him to Hell, or he may forgive him. The faithful will see God in paradise with their bodily eyes, and there will be no distance between them and their creator. All the verses of Qurān are the speech of God and are equal in excellence and greatness.

The Muslims believe in washing the dead with pure water and lotus-tree leaves. After washing, the body is wrapped. If a woman dies, and there is no woman or any man from her near kinsmen or her husband present to wash her, the *tayammum* is performed for her instead of uncovering and wrapping her body. If a man dies and there is no one present except a woman, the tayammum is also performed for him. The tayammum consists of placing the hands once on the soil, rubbing the face with the hands, and rubbing the hands together. It is permissible to touch the soil more than once. The Muslims believe in shrouding the dead in their white Yamani garments, with no shirt or turban. Washing and burial customarily follow promptly at death. In Muslim funeral processions, before viewing the body at the mosque, the mourners walk in front of the bier, as walking behind it is considered a transgression. At the mosque, the mourners cry out "God is most great" four times.

Islam teaches that "We belong to God and to Him we return." The ritual emphasize the tenuous nature of life and respect for the dead. Counseling and support are not part of the tradition. The physician and the health-care team should be alert to provide the necessary intervention in case of severe or prolonged mourning.[3]

Buddhism is a religion that offers each individual a voluntary, idealized way of thought and conduct, based upon an analysis of conditioned existence, dependent upon supreme human effort, and directed toward the realization of freedom in perfect existence. In its historical development and geographical expansion, Buddhism has survived for 25 centuries, in over 30 Asian countries, and has been taught in some 22 Asian languages.

The Buddhists believe that freedom in thought is a prerequisite for freedom in existence. The Buddhist family is taught the principle of tolerance for everyone, and of living so that their thoughts and life are transformed by pure transcendance. They are taught to believe in reincarnation after death, and that a being is nothing but a combination of physical and mental forces or energies. It is believed that what we call death is nothing but the nonfunctioning of physical body, and that will, volition, desire, and thirst continue to exist after death in another form which is called rebirth. They teach that everyone is born, decays, dies, and is reborn. The old man is the continuity of the same series which was the young boy. The difference between death and birth is only a thought–moment. The last thought–moment in this life conditions the first thought–moment in the so-called next life, which, in fact, is the continuity of the same series. During this life itself, too, one thought–moment conditions the next thought–moment. So, from the Buddhist point of view, the question of life after death is not a great mystery, and a Buddhist is never worried about this problem.

Buddhism has profoundly influenced the culture of almost all of East Asia. An important factor in the Buddhist view of death is the doctrine of rebirth. The individual is virtually everlasting, unless and until he attains liberation (Nirvana), when there will be no more rebirth. It is believed that the individual has come through a vast succession of previous existences, and will continue doing that so long as he remains in the grip of craving and spiritual ignorance.

This doctrine does not involve belief in a soul; it does not mean the individual's becoming somehow blissfully eternal; in Nirvana, there is no person, for the person is simply a succession of impermanent states bundled together. At the highest level, one should not hope for individual immortality. The desire for it is a sign that one has not gained the serenity and insight of the saint. The Buddhist believes that just as an individual can gain heavenly or hellish states of existence, he can also become an animal or other living creature. Rebirth is sometimes described in early Buddhist texts as redeath. The problem is not so much that one is going to die and so strives for a salutation which will confer immortality. It is rather than one is condemned to life, which displays its essential unsatisfactoriness by leading to death. The problem is not to gain immortality, but to transcend it; therefore, Nirvana is described as the ''deathless place.'' But it is not deathless, because life goes indefinitely.

In Buddhism, there is no denial of higher or lower realms of existence beyond the plane of this world, nor is there a denial of the gods, even if the doctrine of a Creator is repudiated. Good deeds may lead to an individual's being reborn in heaven; however, this does not constitute final liberation. Heaven, hell, and the great god Brahma, like everything else, are impermanent. They must learn from the Buddha, and through human existence one can hope to attain Nirvana.

The most famous Buddhist parable is the Parable of the Mustard Seed, in which Buddha tells a bereaved mother, who cannot get over the tragic loss of her dead infant son, to search the city for grains of mustard seed from a house in which no one has died. This would be the medicine to cure her condition. But of course, she cannot find such a house. She comes to understand the universality of death, and she goes to the burning-ground to cremate her son.

Because death is the most fearsome sign of the impermanence and ill-fare of the world, there is a great deal of exhortation in the Buddhist tradition to meditate upon death. The most spectacular and gruesome method of meditating on death is for the monk to seat himself at the burning ground, amid the skulls and charred remains. Death is treated not only as an event, but as a symbol of the underlying dissatisfactions of human life.

The Buddhist family is taught to accept death as the chief sign of the impermanence of all hopes. When one neither longs for death nor fears it, he is on the way to transcending both life and death, and gaining the Permanent. For the Buddhist family, mourning may take place quietly and very personally. The Western physician should respect this cultural difference and beware of drawing an inference of pathology in these families.[4] Yamamoto et al. have examined the process of mourning in Japan, where the Shintoist and Buddhist religions sanction the implied presence of the deceased through ancestor worship. Most of 20 Japanese widows interviewed during the acute grief phase of mourning adhered to the cultural beliefs, and were less depressed and anxious and had less difficulty accepting the loss than those who did not. The authors suggested that the almost universal Japanese custom of ancestor worship served an important adaptive function in the work of mourning.[5]

The Hindus believe that the year is analogous to death, and that time destroys the life of mortal beings, and then they die. The Hindus perform the sacrificial rites of the *Agnihotra* (the daily oblation to the god Agni), the new- and full-moon sacrifices, the seasonal offerings, the animal sacrifice, and the Soma sacrifice. By offering these sacrifices, they do not aspire to immortality. They believe that the body does not become immortal either through knowledge or through holy work alone. For the few exceptional persons who have lived many lives of holy work and knowledge, a reunion with the over-soul or God is attained. For most, the fate is to come to life again when they die, and to become the food of Death time after time. Most men and women who depart this world enter the yonder world.

An important ritual for the Hindu is a ceremony in which a dying father bequests his various powers to his son. In this ceremony, a father, when about to die, summons his son. The house is strewn with new grass, the fire is built up, a vessel of water and a dish is placed nearby, and the father, wrapped around with a fresh garment, remains lying. The son lies on top, touching organs with organs. Then the father and son repeat this ritual:

FATHER: "My speech in you I place!"
SON: "Your speech in me I take."
FATHER: "My breath in you I would place!"
SON: "Your breath in me I take."
FATHER: "My eye in you I would place!"
SON:: "Your eye in me I take."
FATHER: "My ear in you I would place!"
SON: "Your ear in me I take."
FATHER: "My tastes in you I would place!"
SON: "Your tastes in me I would take."
FATHER: "My deeds in you I would place!"
SON: "Your deeds in me I take."
FATHER: "My pleasure and pain in you I would place!"
SON: "Your pleasure and pain in me I take."
FATHER: "My bliss, delight, and procreation in you I would place!"
SON: "Your bliss, delight, and procreation in me I take."
FATHER: "My goings in you I would place!"
SON: "Your goings in me I take."
FATHER: "My mind in you I would place!"
SON: "Your mind in me I take."
FATHER: "My intelligence in you I would place!"
SON: "Your intelligence in me I take."

If, however, the father is unable to speak much, he says, "My vital breaths in you I would place!" and the son replies: "Your vital breaths in me I take." Then, as the son leaves, going toward the east, the father calls out after him, "May glory, sacred luster, and fame delight in you!" The son, looking over his left shoulder and hiding his face with his hands, says, "Heavenly worlds and desires do you obtain!"

If the father becomes well, he either dwells under the lordship of his son or wanders as a religious mendicant. If, however, he should die, the son is invested with his father's powers.

The Hindus believe that even if a kinsman died with a relative that that kinsman would be unable to follow the dead relative, and that all excepting his wife are forbidden to follow him on the path of Yama (the god of death). Tomorrow's business should be done today, for death will not wait, whether a person has done it or not. The Hindus believe that man will not die before his time has come, nor will he live after his time is up. They believe that their body will be transformed into another body hereafter, and that their existence is imperishable, perpetual, unchanging, immovable, and without beginning. Knowing the self of man to be such, you must not grieve for the destruction of his body.

The Hindus do not believe in mourning. They believe that the wise man should face death bravely, should not be overcome by pity, tears, or a depressed state of mind. They are taught that the dejection of spirit in this hour of crisis is unknown to men of noble mind, and that wise men do not grieve for the dead or for the living. Knowing men as eternal, all pervading, and unchanging, one should not grieve as man passes from one body to the next.

The Hindus believe that a man of disciplined mind with senses under control attains purity of spirit, which produces an end of all sorrow, and that the intelligence of such a man of pure spirit is soon established in the peace of the self.

Mortality
To death all life of creatures tends.
The early fall to earth is serve,
Of fruits on trees that hand mature.
Of mortals have behold a type;
They, too, succumb, for death when ripe.
As hours fall when long decay
Has worn the posts which formed their stay,
So sink men's frames, when age's course
Has underminded their vital force.
The nights which once have passed away,
and mingled with the morning ray,
Return no more, —as streams which blend
with ocean there forever end.
Revolving ceaseless, night and days
The lives of Mortals wear away;
As summer's torrid solar beams
Dry up the ever lessening streams.
In hours when men at home abide.
Death, too, reposes by their side;
When forth they issue, day by day,

Death walks companion of their way;
Death with them goes when for they roam;
Death with them stays, death brings them me.

Cow dung is used in Hindu houses for purification, and is sprinkled in the house after a death in the family. The Hindus teach that God is in all men and all things, and that in Him we move and have our being. It does not separate life in any smallest detail from religion; it knows what immortality is and has utterly removed from us the reality of death.

Hindu funeral ceremonies are designed to release the dead person from the state of being a ghost, and to send him on his way to the Father's or on to a new reincarnation. Elaborate ceremonies control the rite to passage, especially for the upper classes. The corpse must be cremated; preferably next to a river, into which the ashes are consigned. On the third day, the bones are gathered up and likewise consigned to the river. In succeeding days, offerings are made to the dead person, who now has a ghostly status, and needs nourishment to acquire a subtle body enabling him to travel onward to his next existence. Only after ten days are the relatives who have performed these ceremonies ritually clean, so that they can resume their ordinary activities. The ashes floating downward to the ocean symbolize the way in which all ultimately return to the one divine reality.[6]

This brief overview of the varying religious beliefs which play an important role in the family members' reactions to the death of a loved one hardly does justice to the richness and complexity of the subject. Volumes have been written about this and, as we have pointed out elsewhere in this book, individual and family dynamics are equally, and sometimes more, important variables. Nonetheless, the enigma of religious variations must be appreciated by all of those who attempt to understand and treat families in mourning. It is hoped that the references will provide a source of information for those who wish to do more reading on this subject.

REFERENCES

1. Pynchon T: Gravity's Rainbow. New York, Viking, 1973, p 1
2. Efron B, Maller Rabbi A: Introduction to Judaism. Los Angeles, Cal., Union of American Hebrew Congregations, 1968
3. Williams JA: Islam. New York, Braziller, 1962, pp 104–108

4. Gard RA: Buddhism. New York, Braziller, 1962
5. Yamamoto J et al: Mourning in Japan. Am J Psychiatry 125(June):12, 1969
6. Renou L: Hinduism. New York, Braziller, 1962, pp 30–50, 82–82, 102–105, 130–133, 216–224

Charles E. Hollingsworth
and Robert O. Pasnau

21

Man's Attitudes Toward Death: Funerals and Rituals

Now it's time we were going, I to die and
you to live; but which of us has the happier
prospect is unknown to anyone but God.[1]

Plato

The spectre of death plays a central role in the life of every man. The primal role of death in theology is the subject of the preceding chapter. Socrates, Plato, Hegel, and many other philosophers have written extensively about death. Existentialism holds that man's knowledge of his own mortality is the central core of philosophy. Yet, the significance of death as a cause of mental illness is still a relatively unexplored area, even though man's interest in death is as old as recorded thought.

Our earliest records of man's attitudes toward death go back 4000 years. *The Book of the Dead* from the Egyptian civilization is made up of various prayers, psalms, and incantations that were written on papyrus and left with the dead. Some of the writings in this collection date from early predynastic cultures, so that the attitudes expressed are at least 5000 years old. The Egyptians were so thoroughly convinced of a life after death that they buried hundreds of slaves with their dead kings to serve them in a life thereafter. This terrible procedure was later modified so that pictures or symbols of slaves were put in the tombs of the kings.[2]

Frazer wrote that all known primitive peoples are so certain of immortality that they do not even raise the question of any alternative.[3] Some Indian tribes believe in a life after death while one is waiting to be reincarnated. The Egyptians believed that it was possible to die again in the life hereafter. Documented doubting as to a life thereafter was first presented by the Greeks. Plato's *Republic* contains a long description of the next world by a man who supposedly died and came back to life.[4]

None of us handle the loss of loved ones easily or well. Those who are impressed with a child's seeming lack of involvement when a death occurs in the family must take a second look. The loss of loved ones, especially through death, is one of the most important precipitants of major mental illness. These illnesses may start immediately after the death of a loved one, or they may appear much later in life. Children who lose loved ones—mothers, fathers, or siblings—in their early childhood are profoundly affected by this. The child's emotional development may be damaged, leading to serious mental illness in adult life. Perhaps a major difference between the effect of death on children as compared with adults is that children are unprepared to deal with it. In addition, children tend to be more emotionally vulnerable than are adults, and this may be another reason why the reverberations from such a trauma are more damaging.

Perhaps only when we lose a loved one, and identify very intensely with the death and burial, do we become fully aware of the fact that his body will decompose under the earth, and possibly it is only then that we fully comprehend the reality and the inevitability of our own end. Whether or not there is a life after death, man's need to believe that his soul lives on after his body decomposes is a most primitive and important one. There seems to be no substitute for the reassurance that comes from such a belief.

The American's reaction to a family member's death has changed with the times. A hundred years ago, when someone in a village died, the bell tolled for the whole town. The family watched the labored breathing cease, carried the body to the church, and, after the service, buried their loved one in the churchyard.

Today, the community of the living has been separated from the dying. Dying has lost its intimacy. Often nowadays the loved one is kept alive for long periods of time, maintained by artificial ventilators in impersonal, stressful intensive-care units, where the family members' visits are very restricted. Many patients are resuscitated long after the family has given up hope because the hospital staff is so involved with saving lives at any cost that they overlook the needs and feelings of the family. Sometimes the staff makes the incorrect assumption that the family would want the patient maintained indefinitely by artificial means.

During the 1970s our American culture is re-evaluating its attitudes toward death and the ritual associated with burial or cremation. The trend in funerals is toward more participation, as compared to observation. Changes include a variety of funeral practices and styles, growing impatience with traditional approaches to death by those who find them empty, proliferating help agencies for the dying and bereaved, and counseling and grief work which increasingly focus upon integrating the experience of dying into the process of living.

More humanistic funeral ceremonies are becoming popular, with services written in advance by the deceased, or by close family members or friends. "Hot lines" are being developed to offer free counseling to the terminally ill and their families. Many families have found that if the members participate in planning for the actual burial, they are able to begin the mourning process without delay.

In the face of spiraling funeral costs, more than 120 funeral or memorial societies in the United States and Canada are seeking to reduce funeral costs and to press for dignified and simple services. According to information from the National Funeral Directors Association, Americans paid an average of $1117 for an adult funeral in 1973, plus an additional $750 for burial plots and such items as outer shields for the coffin. The cheapest funeral cost about $200.[5] The largest variable between inexpensive and expensive funerals is the price of the coffin.

Not until this century did the average person begin to add expensive frills to death. The Old Testament Book of Jeremiah, chapter 22, verse 19, indicates that it was a disgrace for one to be buried in a crude manner, yet the Jewish customs out of which Christian practices grew never put much emphasis on elaborate burial. It was considered an honor to be buried with one's ancestors. According to the National Funeral Directors Association, the number of cremations in the United States has remained nearly constant between 1960 and 1975, amounting to about 5% of all funerals. Cremations in California and the Pacific Coast are increasing, with half of all cremations in the United States occurring there.[5] Funeral and memorial societies often arrange low-cost cremations, with the average cost being $250 for the entire affair. Some funeral and memorial societies specialize in cremation followed by disposal of the ashes at sea—an ancient Scandinavian custom. These groups emphasize dignity and simplicity.

Religious affiliation influences the decision for cremation or burial. Ancient Judaism practiced earth burial and used cremation only in exceptional circumstances. Although the Bible does not prohibit cremation, it was not regularly practiced in Biblical times. Cremation was used only to dispose of large numbers of bodies after battles or catastrophes and to handle the bodies of executed criminals. The three modern branches of Judaism differ on cremation. The Orthodox tradition is very explicit in its opposition to cremation, basing it upon ancient scriptural precedent and Talmudic teaching. In general, this resistance is shared by Conservative Jewish congregations. Reform Judaism does not regard burial as mandatory and has no opposition to cremation. The early Christian church followed Jewish practice. Roman Catholic opposition to cremation continued to until the 1960s, when the Second Vatican Council authorized priests to participate in cremation when requested to do so. Catholics are now permitted cremation, although burial is preferred. Most Protestant denominations leave this decision to individual choice. A few extremely conservative groups reject cremation, usually on the grounds that the Bible teaches a literal interpretation of the resurrection of the body.

Traditional funeral rites are being challenged by an increasing number of Americans who hold no religious preference. Some choose a secular memorial service, others a modified religious service, and some, no service at all. Some prefer a humanist approach, which provides a service that does not deal in religious imagery and language, but lifts people up socially and psychologically. Because there are valuable functions which the funeral can fulfill, many families want a funeral but feel that any religious content would be hypocritical because they have had no prior commitment to it.

Even traditional funerals are more flexible. Since 1971, the Catholic Church has used a new funeral rite. One change allows a nonpracticing Catholic to have a scripture service. Formerly, such a person could be denied the one standard practice, the Requiem Mass, as well as church burial. The new rite is a recognition that the time of death is not the time to judge, and it replaces the old notion that if you didn't go to church when alive, that you should not receive a Christian burial. A growing number of nontraditional services of all faiths include those in which lay persons write poetry, inspirational thoughts, and eulogies for friends, relatives, and even themselves. Those who favor this type of service feel that the ceremonies lend a personal touch and greater meaning. These alternative ceremonies may be held in parks and gardens—not merely at a cemetery graveside. Often the family may choose a location which has had meaning for the family and the deceased loved one.

For church-oriented families, the trend is toward funerals inside the church sanctuary as well as memorial services, usually held in church a few days or even weeks after interment. There is a trend away from the private, "family only" funeral to one in which many friends, colleagues, and casual acquaintances are included. It has been recognized that families often need the support of many organizations in the community during bereavement. This community support is living evidence to the family that they can move through this event and have emotional support during the mourning process.

Funeral customs vary throughout the country. Viewing the body at the funeral home the night before seems to be practiced most in the Midwest. On the East Coast, two viewing nights are often scheduled, the first for the immediate family, and the second for family and friends. Another Midwest custom is the church pot-luck meal following the graveside service. This helps relieve the stark abandonment at the end of the service when everyone would otherwise go his separate way. In the Southeast, neighbors bring quantities of food to the home of the deceased and visit in large numbers. There is a recent trend to view the deceased body at the mortuary, but in the past and in many families at the present time, the deceased member's body is returned to the home on the day before the funeral, and friends and relatives visit to view the body and the flowers. Several friends or family members hold a wake and stay up in the room with the body all night. The funeral is held the following day, with much thought given to the order of cars in the procession from the home to the church or gravesite. Passengers are assigned so as to be respectful to the nuclear family, the extended family, and the friends. After a church service there is usually a brief graveside service. The family is usually visited at home after the services by relatives and the closest personal friends.

In the liberal Reform branch of Judaism, there is a move toward "reality" in funerals and confronting death, and more Jewish families hold funerals in the temple, as part of the idea that the temple is involved in the cycle of life. If you name your baby in the temple, are bar mitzvahed, married, and confirmed there, then it makes sense to round out the life cycle by holding the funeral in the temple.

There remains the need for the profession of undertaking. Even today, grief-stricken families are automatically considered to be in the market for the following "services."

1. Removal of the body to a funeral home and, subsequently, transportation from the funeral home to the cemetery or crematorium.
2. Embalming, a process in which the blood is removed from the dead body with the substitution of a chemical replacement.
3. Cosmetic work, the decoration of the face and other visible parts of the deceased with powder and paint to restore a lifelike appearance; the arrangement of features into a cheerful appearance and styling of the hair.
4. The use of the funeral home facilities, including "viewing room" and chapel.
5. The services of the funeral director and his staff in obtaining burial permits and death certificates, placing obituary notices in the newspapers, scheduling church services, receiving and displaying flowers, arranging for pallbearers and hearse, and providing a limousine for the family.

Coffins are usually the most expensive single items in funerals. Their cost ranges from $50 cloth-covered wooden boxes to steel and bronze monuments costing thousands of dollars wholesale. The smallest expenses come in the way of "extras," and sometimes may not be mentioned in the funeral director's estimate of funeral costs to the bereaved. Some of these "extras" are transportation when the funeral home is beyond a "fixed-service" radius from the cemetery, a flower car in the funeral procession, and services of an organist and minister. Besides this, the cemetery plot is an extra expense and may be very costly.

Recently, the U.S. government has had to intervene to prevent some of the most serious consumer fraud in which funeral directors play on the guilt of the bereaved. Federal legislation is being drafted which attempts to implement fair practices in an industry which has been charged with deplorable misrepresentation and heavy sell of grief-stricken families at their most vulnerable moment. The cost to these families and to society may be very great. A few clergymen are refusing to take part in any funeral services conducted in commercial funeral homes because of the added expenses for the bereaved, and also because they believe that a funeral should concentrate on the memories of the person when he was alive.

Part of the counseling experience of many ministers we contacted has been directed towards the goal of supporting and reassuring the bereaved families after their upsetting experiences with the occasional unscrupulous funeral director, who considers it part of his job to elicit every possible bit of guilt and remorse in the family. These clergymen believe that the commercial funeral should be discouraged, and that the memorial service should be substituted in its place. A memorial service is directed towards the people who are left alive, a symbol of the immortality of friendship and love between people and their friends, their children, and their extended families.

The authors believe that a meaningful memorial service should consist of

1. The Tribute, soft classical or other appropriate music for about five minutes
2. The Memorial, silent meditation for two minutes
3. The Eulogy, limited to five minutes and delivered by a close friend
4. The Response, a poem written by a close friend especially for the occasion or a favorite poem of the deceased

Some of the most rewarding memorial services the authors have attended have been held in the Botanical Gardens near our hospital, a lovely setting where many on our staff have spent pleasant times in solitary walks and meditation.

It is the belief of the authors that some form of ritual is required to begin the process of saying good-bye to the deceased loved one and that such experiences facilitate the mourning process.

REFERENCES

1. Plato: The Apology. Cambridge, Mass., Harvard University Press, 1953, p 145
2. Toynbee A: Man's Concern With Death. New York, McGraw–Hill, 1968
3. Frazer JG: Death and resurrection: the rhythm of nature. *In* Gaster TH (ed): The New Golden Bough. New York, Criterion, 1959, pp 223–224
4. Plato: The Republic. New York, Blac, 1942, pp 221–477
5. See C: The End Game. LA Times West Magazine, Oct. 8, 1972, pp 24–26

Charles E. Hollingsworth
and Robert O. Pasnau

22

Visiting the Family After the Death of a Loved One

The family in mourning should not be forgotten or neglected in the weeks and months after a death, but should be visited, called, and written at frequent intervals to provide emotional support while they are in grief and mourning, and while they are making necessary adjustments in their family structure.

The physician should phone the family the day following the death to extend his sympathy and to offer any resources he or the hospital may have for emotional support to the family during the mourning period. This phone call will help the family feel that their loved one's final hours were attended by a warm, considerate, and caring physician.

If the physician's relationship with the family or spouse was close, he may wish to provide the bereaved person with a series of supportive home visits or office visits during the first several months of grief; the doctor can offer help that is far superior to a prescription for drugs. Because grief-stricken persons rarely seek help spontaneously, the physician should take the initiative by visiting the home of the bereaved during the first or second evening after the death. At this time, the physician can answer questions about the final illness that frequently concern other family members. He can help the bereaved by talking privately with him about the need for the normal grief and mourning process, which should not be postponed in order to give the appearance of the tower of strength for those other grief-stcicken family members. He should advise against daytime tranquilizers that friends or family members may recommend, and, most importantly, he should urge the bereaved to see him in his office three or four days later. The home visit may prove to be a time saver in the long run for the busy physician and is an excellent way to initiate periodic follow-up visits for the bereaved. To make this home visit, the physician must master his own guilt or anxiety over the death of the deceased, i.e., guilt or anxiety that may be especially troubling because the dead person had been in his care.

The physician and other health professionals should feel comfortable in sending sympathy cards to bereaved families with whom they have worked closely. These prove to be very meaningful to the survivors, who feel the same nurturing attitudes that were part of the nursing care of their loved one.

The physician should schedule an appointment with the immediate family of the deceased when the autopsy report is complete, to discuss the findings in simple, understandable laymen's terms. He should encourage the family to ask questions and request more explanation. This meeting may be able to answer questions which had concerned the family about the cause of death or the possibility that they too might be afflicted with the same disease. Most families appreciate the physician taking the initiation for arranging such a meeting, since this strengthens their belief that the physician has nothing to hide and is being frank and candid with them.

The physician should encourage family members to seek professional counseling or therapy during the mourning process if they feel that their reaction is more intense, prolonged, distorted, or delayed than what they consider normal or what those around them consider normal. From a preventative point of view, it is better to obtain a psychiatric consultation early in an effort to actualize a normal grief reaction, than to postpone any action until the reaction is so severe that months of therapy are required to bring about a successful resolution of the conflict.

If the family has any religious affiliation, they usually welcome visits from their minister, priest, or rabbi. For all families, but especially those that are not religious, much strength is derived from the emotional support of their friends and relatives. In these times of crisis, our memories and friends will get us through. Close friends and relatives can provide much-needed emotional support after a death in the family. The most important role of a close friend is as listener rather than as adviser.

So often when several friends have gathered at the family's home, they tend to forget that this is a house in mourning and begin to talk louder, tell jokes, or display joy about seeing friends or relatives who have not been seen for years. It is not necessary to be gloomy, but it is courteous to show respect for the immediate family by being quiet while inside the home. So often flowers and food brought to the family's home show love at a time when it is difficult to find the words that convey our sympathy. This is a tradition in many cultures.

A visit to a family in mourning should not be lengthy—thirty minutes to an hour is usually enough. The immediate family needs some time to be alone.

In some customs, visitors go to the family's home immediately after the funeral service or sometime during the afternoon. If the home is crowded at this time, one should make the visit very short, express sympathy to the family, leave graciously, and plan to visit later that week or that evening. At no time should the house of mourning become excessively noisy.

Physicians may be very helpful to friends or relatives by sharing with them some of the simple guidelines stated in this chapter. In all cases, the physician's visit is something that is never forgotten by the family in mourning.

Charles E. Hollingsworth
and Robert O. Pasnau

23

Psychotherapy for the Bereaved

"Give sorrow words, the grief that does not
speak
knits up the o'erwrought breast and bids it
break."

Shakespeare (Macbeth IV, iii, 208)

There has been a great deal of emphasis recently on the use of therapeutic intervention resources to assist the family in grief and mourning, as evidenced by the many seminars and scores of new books on
death, dying, grief, and mourning. These are very helpful to the
mourning individual and the dying person for identifying and coping
with attitudes toward death. The dying person needs a sympathetic and
understanding person to talk with about his feelings. Adequate resolution of these feelings can bring peace and serenity to the dying patient.
A patient can mature psychologically when dying just as in any other
stage of life and development.

When an energetic, loving young father learned that his illness was
terminal, he decided to swim out into the ocean near his home, look
back and remember for the last time the beautiful memories of his wife

and children, and then fill his lungs with water. The alternative for him was hospitals, pain, becoming a patient instead of a person, being reduced to something less than a man who could swim out to meet his death. But he changed his mind. Having suffered little physical pain during his life, he felt it would be cowardly to avoid it in dying. Against the advice of doctors, who recommended chemotherapy and radiation treatments, he went home to die. He talked with his wife. His son taught him how to play the guitar. And he began to write a short book on his life and dying. Appreciation of daily experiences increased. The sounds of Bach and Rachmaninoff, the taste of food, the feel of the sand and the wind, and the warmth in his sons' eyes all filled his heart with joy. He looked inward, reviewing and evaluating himself and his relationships with others. He looked outward, and his love ripened. One night he died quietly and peacefully in his sleep, content that he had not drowned the best part of his life.

In a similar way, bereaved families need someone to talk to as well. Death is a crisis for the family. When a death has occurred, not only must each surviving individual bear the pain of grief and adjust to the loss; the surviving family as a whole must do so as well. There are specific family readjustment tasks that complement one another.

It is not difficult to understand why death is a crisis for the family. It fulfills the criterion for a crisis described as a situation which "cannot be easily handled by the family's commonly used problem-solving mechanisms, but forces the employment of novel patterns. These are necessarily within the range of the family's capacities, but may be patterns never called into operation in the past."[1] Two characteristics of death make it readily convertible into a crisis situation. One is its stark finality—the irretrievable loss of a human being. One cannot replace the loss, but only adjust to it. The second is that because death is not a frequent occurrence one usually has little prior experience in dealing with it, and therefore must seek a new solution when it does occur. Death is perceived by the family as a severe hardship and as a threatening crisis.

The death of a family member is often an unanticipated crisis which may be perceived as a threat, a loss, or a challenge associated with intense feelings. Just as the individual must deal with his emotional response to death by intrapsychic adjusting processes, the family's reactions to death are handled by intrafamilial processes involving interactions between groups of individuals working though their grief. The family's readjustment, in turn, further affects the resolution of individual family members' mourning.

According to Hill, three variables determine whether a stress event results in a crisis for the family: "(1) the hardships of the situation or event itself; (2) the resources of the family; its role structure, flexibility, and previous history with crisis; and (3) the definition the family makes of the event; that is, whether members treat the event as if it were or as if it were not a threat to their status, goals and objectives."[2]

The family's task after the death of a loved one is to give permission for the grief process to proceed by encouraging the various members to mourn and express their feelings. In our culture crying is too often represented as weakness, implying that one should be strong. Many family members try to avoid both the internal distress connected with the grief experience and the necessary expression of emotion. Permitting family members to mourn says, in effect, "We are all hurting. Let us suffer our pain together." Members can help one another. The family must first work through the grief of individual members. As other members become cognizant of the psychological steps of mourning, their own grieving may begin. Families with effective communication systems are better prepared to cope with the stress of a death.

Crisis intervention with bereaved families is a very useful method of prevention of psychiatric disorders or medical illnesses.[1] Many families need professional help in delineating and establishing effective communication between the various members whose relationships may have been severely stressed during a lengthy illness of a loved one.

Since it is obvious that all bereaved persons cannot be seen by a psychiatrist, it is important that other mental health professionals and clergymen understand the mourning process and family dynamics during this crisis. Hackett has written the following guidelines for working with the bereaved in normal grief situations[3]:

1. Encourage ventilation (through tears, anguish-even hostility, if needed).
2. Emphasize naturalness and need for such reactions.
3. Prescribe minor tranquilizers if restlessness and anxiety are severe during working hours. However, minor tranquilizers and sedatives should not be used in an attempt to spare the person the intense feelings during the normal grief and mourning process. A delayed grief reaction can be caused by such sedation or tranquilized treatment.
4. Prescribe minor tranquilizers to overcome persistent insomnia. Do not prescribe barbiturates or other 'sleeping-pills' because of the risk of suicide in these bereaved families.
5. Do not prescribe antidepressant medication for normal grief situations.

In abnormal grief situations, or if symptoms last more than five months without clear improvement, the physician should immediately consider and arrange for a consultation by a psychiatrist or other health professional.

The process of mourning as a reaction to the real loss of a loved person must be carried to completion. The attachments are unresolved as long as the affective process of mourning has not been accomplished. The flight from or denial of suffering of grief is but a temporary gain, because the necessity to mourn persists in the psychic apparatus. Deutsch states that the inner rejection of painful experience is always active, especially in childhood, and the general tendency toward "unmotivated" depressions is the subsequent expression of emotional reactions which were once withheld and have since remained in latent readiness for discharge.[4]

In determining the chances of a good response to insight psychotherapy, one must assess the stability of human relationships and of work situations, the ability to bear painful affects and to relate to the therapist, intelligence, motivation for treatment, and the capacity for introspection and insight. In bereaved patients experiencing a pathological grief reaction, briefer forms of uncovering therapy may be quite effective in freeing the patient from his/her conflict in relieving him/her of the symptoms.

The decision to employ insight psychotherapy for patients with depressive neuroses should be based on the presence of those criteria, referable to ego functions, that indicate the likelihood of a good response to such therapy, regardless of symptoms. The sensitive, dependent, ambivalent patient often does not have the capacity to respond to insight therapy, and can best be helped by supportive measures. In patients experiencing a pathological grief reaction when grief work has been blocked by unresolved aggression toward the lost person, careful uncovering of the initially unconscious anger in the course of insight psychotherapy can thaw out the emotional freeze and enable the patient to express both his anger and his grief, and thus to lose the depressive symptoms that have formed a part of his pathological reaction.

The achievement of insight into the world around him and into himself is one of the great achievements of man as a species and as a biological and culture-oriented organism. He has come to know that a stringent, critical, but affectionate self-scrutiny, as well as an outwardly directed scrutiny, can lead to a greater development and growth of his individual and his creative potential. In the development of the individual, new insights independent of psychotherapy are valuable.

Also, as part of psychotherapy, new and accurate insights can be the basis for significant steps forward.

Psychotherapy has designed specific techniques for achieving goals which one sets when a person enters psychotherapy or as treatment progresses. The major goal for the bereaved who is experiencing a pathological, distorted, or delayed grief reaction is to appropriately work through those emotions and defense mechanisms which have prevented appropriate resolution of the grief and loss, with resumption to a stable life-style following certain readjustments which are realistically based on the person's world without the deceased. After therapy, both the therapist and the patient should evaluate the progress in terms of achievement of previously specified goals.

Whereas the goal of insight-oriented therapy is the resolution of selected conflicts, usually related to the bereavement and limited removal of pathological defenses with secondary relief of symptoms, in supportive therapy the goal is more limited. It is usually formulated as the restoration of prior equilibrium and reduction of anxiety and fear in new situations, with help in tolerating unalterable situations. The therapy offers support by an authority figure during the crisis or temporary decompensation of pathological grief. It also has the goal of restoring or strengthening the defenses and integrative capacities that have been impaired. It provides a period of acceptance and dependence for a patient who is acutely in need of help in dealing with his guilt, his shame, or his anxiety, and in meeting the frustrations or the external pressures that have been too great for him to handle.

The success of the readjustment period is determined by the degree to which it is permissible to express feelings of sadness and loss, as well as the less acceptable reactions of anger, guilt, and relief. The progress of grief work can be evaluated on the basis of (1) the passage through the various stages of normal grief, (2) the successful resolution of the mourning process in such a way as to imply that the deceased will remain a "living memory" without the pain that originally accompanies the grief reaction, and (3) the development or identification of morbid grief reactions which indicate unresolved mourning.

It is painful and difficult to give up the memory of the deceased family member as a force in family activities; but this must be done and can be slowly and gradually accomplished. Some families live "as if the lost member were still with them" and then gradually taper off this idea as it ceases to be a felt need. Some family members may argue over conflicting interpretations of what the deceased family member would have said or wanted, each member quoting his authority to rationalize his own desires. The family, respecting and cherishing the memory of the departed, will eventually be able to make decisions based on what will best meet its present needs without continually invoking what the departed might have said or done.

After a death in a family there is a realignment of intrafamilial roles because a role has been left vacant. Death creates a change in the composition of the family group, with a redistribution of responsibility and needs. Socioemotional functions such as socialization of family members and children, economic support, and maintenance of physical needs must be redistributed. These socioemotional functions of the family involve such affects as giving and receiving love in the family.

Realignment of intrafamilial roles is especially difficult and evident for the problems in the one-parent family created by the death of a mother or father. Such widowed parents find it difficult to fulfill the role of both mother and father for their children and provide continuing support for the family. This activity may involve living on various death benefits or seeking a substitute or additional means of support, such as the wife or oldest child going to work. The surviving spouse also must attempt to provide the children with love previously given by two persons and satisfying his or her own emotional needs without a spouse. This leads to increased family solidarity and support. Eventually a new person may be introduced to the family; temporarily, if the spouse begins to date or in the instance of a Big Brother to facilitate the role modeling for a son whose father is deceased, or permanently, if the widowed spouse decides to remarry.

After the death of a family member, there is a realignment of the family to the organizations and institutions comprising the social system with which various family members are affiliated. A widowed wife's membership in the couple's club at church or the son's participation on a father-and-son baseball team are some examples which come to mind. Family members can adjust and adapt, either by continuation in present activities or by seeking activities better suited for one's new status. The widowed parent may withdraw from the couple's club and join Parents Without Partners, or continue in the couples club and find a suitable escort. The son whose father is deceased may ask an uncle or other family member or family friend to participate in the Little League with him. Some reactions of family members to a death in the family are indicative of successful family readjustment, whereas others indicate dysfunctional interaction. It is possible to evaluate how well the family copes with stress and provide professional emotional support during these times by carefully looking at how these problems are handled.

The major interactional adjustment for the family to the death of a member is role change with the reestablishment of a new equilibrium wihin the family. Roles must be reorganized and decisions must be made about who will assume what responsibilities. One variable is the number of roles held by the member who died. Another is the type of role he fulfilled. The process of readjustment is more difficult for the family which has lost a father who occupied several important roles than for the family which has lost a baby. It is important for family members to appropriate vital roles and functions of the deceased in a just and equitable manner according to individual need, ability, and potential. The well-adjusted family has a built-in process which makes role assumption explicit and well understood by all family members and reallocates the role functions of the deceased with minimal difficulty. The well-adjusted family has both a good communication system as well as prior equitable role allocation.

Three variables which characterize families that are able to cope with crisis events are involvement, integration, and adaptation. Role reorganization refers to the process of adaptation in which the family group and each of its members can change their responses to one another and the world around them as the situation demands by flexibility of the family in group structure and individual behavior.[5]

Unfortunately, many families are not characterized by a balanced apportionment of roles, and in these families there may be tension based upon the roles of the scapegoated and the generator of conflict within the family. If the member who died was a scapegoat in the family, readjustment following this loss must take into account his purpose within the economy of the family. The scapegoating role may be reassigned, and if roles cannot be realigned to incorporate a scapegoating function, the threat of collapse occurs. If, however, the death was that of a member who produced conflict and tension within the family, such as a chronic alcoholic, the result may be increased family solidarity, because of the removal of a divisive element. If the member who died occupied a position not seen as crucial by the rest of the family, and if the family perceived the deceased person as the one who "was always a little different, and never quite fit in," then readjustment is minimal and may proceed without much difficulty. This is seen especially in families where a very elderly invalid aunt of one of the spouses had been living at home with the family.

Increased solidarity in the family experiencing the death of one of its members is an important reaction of the family to death. In many ways, trouble brings individuals together, and the family is united by the loss. This increased solidarity gives needed emotional support to all members at a crucial time and insures the successful functioning of the newly reconstituted family unit. If the marriage is a solid one, spouses are able to achieve greater closeness in facing the death of their child. Solidarity can also result when a member who caused conflict dies.

Solidarity requires consensus regarding role reorganization, and family members must come to some understanding as to how the roles will be filled and by whom.[5] If agreement cannot be reached, roles are left unfulfilled, overlap unnecessarily, and possibly conflict. In the family more advanced in its life cycle, the potential for disagreement increases because children have a greater voice in family matters by virtue of being older and of being future or present income producers who can be tapped for support. Some reasons for conflict are: continuation of conflict regarding role definition prior to death of a member; several persons able and willing to assume the same role; lack of clarity as to what the role entails and whether the deceased person had fulfilled a role which kept hostilities and conflict dormant, or at least under control in the family. In the family in which the spouses are bound by the child in a tenuous relationship, the child's death usually exacerbates serious marital conflict.

The death of a child is viewed with much sadness because life has been cut so short for this human being. Parents deal with this loss by investing additional emotional energy in the remaining children or by having another child, especially if the deceased was an only child. This type of object replacement also occurs when a widowed spouse remarries. If parents or a widow have adequately worked through their grief, they are ready to accept a replacement. If they have not successfully completed the work of grief, the replacement child or spouse may be forced to live in the image of the deceased child or spouse. In cases of unresolved mourning, there are often frequent comparisons, imposition of the identify of the deceased upon the substitute, and even unconscious identification of the two. Frequently, surviving or replacment children are overprotected and restricted by parents whose fears for this child become unrealistically exaggerated. These children often have morbid preoccupations which may lead to personality difficulties for them. If the spouse is being replaced, personality damage would probably not result from object replacement, because an adult is more capable than a child of protesting the molding of his personality to the image of the deceased.

During bereavement, one may experience loss, guilt, anger, a sense of relief, anxiety, a feeling of helplessness or powerlessness, hostility, and/or fear. Some experience all of these; others experience only some of them, and these emotions may occur simultaneously or in any sequence. During bereavement one comes to grips with these feelings and, having worked the grief through, is no longer overcome by these emotions. Parents often feel guilty for not having recognized sooner that their child was sick. They sometimes feel that if they had taken the child to the doctor sooner they might have saved the child's life. If mourning proceeds successfully, the parent realized he did all that was possible, and the sense of guilt is relieved. If the parent continues to accuse himself in an intense and bitter manner, a severe mourning reaction ensues. Mourning can be viewed as pathological if the feelings of loss, guilt, anger, relief, anxiety, helplessness, hostility, or fear are excessively intense or violent, or if the process of mourning is unduly prolonged.[5]

The family may displace its guilt and anger over the death and create the role of scapegoat, which may involve the relationship between both parents and a surviving child in the family. Parents or other family members may experience guilt for several reasons: an ambivalent relationship with the dead child marked by some hostility; a previous wish for him to die, experienced, perhaps, in a moment of anger, but now recalled and unrealistically interpreted as leading to death; a feeling of anger at the deceased for dying; and the wish that more had been given of oneself while the deceased was living. If the child has died through some real carelessness or failure on the part of the parents to secure his safety, the reaction of guilt can be especially severe.

Some parents handle their guilt over a death by bitterly accusing the doctor of not giving proper treatment to the child, or they blame God, or they may even become angry toward a remaining child who does not realize why he is being so treated. Parents sometimes use the surviving child as the scapegoat or as a means of relieving or preventing them from facing guilt. The scapegoating may take the form of the parents's being annoyed at a surviving child and continually finding fault with whatever he does. The parents may even actively blame him for the sibling's death. Unless the adults can come to grips with these feelings, the child is likely to remain a scapegoat.

Other family members can displace guilt and hostility toward each other. Spouse may blame spouse, especially when the child's illness and death may be based upon genetic transmission, as in the family discussed at length in Part I of this volume. If previous family relationships included a scapegoat, then the re-establishment of a scapegoat may be a way of re-achieving homeostasis. Here, the scapegoat role may be reassigned, and if roles cannot be realigned to include the scapegoating function in the operational dynamics of the family, there occurs the threat of family turmoil, conflict, or even collapse of the nuclear family.

Mourning is of longer duration in anticipatory grief, but of lower intensity. Conversely, mourning may not be as extended if grief was precipitated by a sudden loss, but is of greater intensity. When the death of a loved one is anticipated for weeks, months, or even a year or two in advance, the mourner is not spared the necessity of having to complete his grief work, but "the shock and suddenness is lacking, and as a result the potential, at least for intensity, lowers."[5] In such instances, some of the grief work will have occurred by the time of death and the reaction may be one of relief, especially if the dying individual was suffering. If it is an adult who is dying, anticipatory grief allows the family to consult with the dying member regarding what they should do; for example, a husband can advise his wife to sell his business and use the money to send the children to college. Thus, the dying individual can share in the preparatory mourning and even facilitate it. Most families view this as a powerful family-emotional experience, in which mourning becomes a gradual, extended, and less intense process.[5]

Family therapy should be considered when the pathological grief reaction is caused by or is a symptom of a pathological family interaction. This treatment modality was first described in the mid-1950s by a number of clinicians and theoreticians, working independently, who were associated with its beginnings. Bateson, Jackson,[6] and their colleagues in Palo Alto had coined the phrase "double bind," which referred to the conflicting messages which children sometimes receive, usually from their mothers, creating situations in which they cannot win regardless of what they do. Although this concept is used to understand the relationship which is thought to exist between schizophrenic patients and their families, it was later proposed that children who grow up in even relatively healthy homes are sometimes caught in the double bind. This concept has been of major importance in understanding family problems.[6] Wynne and his colleagues at the National Institute of Mental Health used the concept "pseudomutuality" to describe a rigid family system in which individual growth and divergence from established roles is not tolerated. The primary concern is the preservation of the status quo of the family and its facade of harmony and well-being.[7] Ackerman presented a conceptual model in his 1956 paper, "Interlocking Pathology in Family Relationships," and also developed a therapeutic method which he called "family therapy."[8] Bowen described the "undifferentiated family ego mass" and developed a therapeutic method which he called "family psychotherapy."[9] During this period, Satir taught family dynamics to psychiatric residents at the Illinois State Psychiatric Institute in Chicago. Her book, *Conjoint Family Therapy*, which was published several years later, was based largely on her course outlines.[10] Bell claimed to be the first to use this new method as a form of treatment for the entire family.[11] Minuchin and others stressed the importance of viewing the family from a systems approach.[12]

Whether they approached family interaction from the standpoint of studying the process of interaction in families, or whether they approached it as a specific method of treatment for the family, all of these pioneers agreed on at least one thing: They viewed the family itself as a viable entity. Essentially they all described the family as a system that is constantly changing, sometimes slowly, sometimes rapidly. It is a system that is delicately balanced and struggles to maintain that balance, or "homeostasis." Sometimes the balance reflects family pathology, and in the course of therapy the balance hopefully is changed. The system is made up of subsystems (i.e., the individual, family members), and a change in one part changes the balance of the system. This description challenged the assumptions of other methods of treatment in that by changing an individual member, the entire family would necessarily benefit.

Family group therapy is an effort to effect changes within a total family through a series of conferences attended by the parents, the children nine years of age and older, and the therapist. The therapeutic goals are family-centered, rather than person-centered. The primary intent of the therapist is to accomplish a modification of the functioning and structure of the family as a group. It is assumed that as a consequence, modifications will be effectuated secondarily in the situation of individuals within the family. The method of the therapy emerges, then, from the one basic assumption differentiating it from individual therapy: The family is the unit to be treated. It is important to stress that in this method the family is not regarded as an assembly of individuals, but is recognized as a biological and social unit. One must keep in mind that here no child or parent is under treatment as an individual.

Termination of therapy is a very complex matter in cases in which the patient or family is being treated for a pathological grief reaction, or even after a normal grief reaction following the death of a loved one. In brief psychotherapy, termination is often an explicit issue from the outset. There has been very little written about termination for any form of psychotherapy, but even less written about termination following treatment for a pathological grief reaction. The French saying expresses it well: "Partir c'est mourir un peu"—"To part is to die a little." Terminating psychotherapy inevitably has its painful aspects, whether the termination is positively determined by the happy accomplishment of goals or whether it represents a sad acknowledgement of failure to achieve the desired results.

In those instances in which one thoughtfully concludes, after careful and thorough consideration, that therapy is not going to be effective, one should make the termination as supportive as possible, with suggestions of alternate strategies to cope with the problem. For the bereaved person who has not resolved his distorted or pathological grief reaction, premature termination may intensify the feeling of loss, self-pity, and anxiety. Even with successful resolution of one's symptoms, much time must be spent, during the working through of the termination covering several different sessions, discussing the meaning of termination as it relates to the previous loss.

The criterion for termination, whether symptomatic improvement, which may be conceived of as a consequence of a flight into health, transference cure, resolution of conflict, or the result of specific effective interventions, should be a focus of rigorous investigation by the therapist, necessitating much discussion of this issue between patient and therapist. A decision must be made as to whether to aim for an absolute ending of the therapeutic contact, or offer the patient the option of subsequent visits, or definitely plan them. It diminishes the painful loss that the bereaved person experiences if, upon terminating with a therapist, he is told that he may call to reestablish contact or come in during future crisis situations. Often the patient will request one or two visits during intense emotional periods at the time of anniversary reactions.

Another consideration is whether to proceed with the same schedule until the last visit or to offer additional support by terminating gradually. Regardless of the criteria for termination and the various approaches to it, therapists should remember that this is an emotionally charged experience for the person who has experienced a pathological grief reaction, even though the patient may minimize the significance of the separation, because it may symbolically recapitulate the death of the loved one. It is generally best to agree upon a termination date sometime in the future, thereby permitting anticipatory psychotherapeutic work about separation feelings. Frequently, these feelings are not expressed directly, but appear in other forms, such as regression to old patterns. A fight may be provoked with the therapist because it does not hurt as much to leave somebody with whom you are angry. The absence of separation may represent a failure to communicate about something vital, or it may indicate that the bereaved person has been successfully disengaging long before the agreement to terminate was specifically stipulated. In a similar way, many persons use anticipatory grief to begin and sometimes even complete the mourning process when their loved one has a prolonged terminal illness. The bereaved person's expressed eagerness to end therapy should never be accepted as an indication that there is no accompanying anxiety about separation.

Termination should only be considered when the patient has the capacity to tolerate separation and loss in a state of positive identification with the therapist. As termination approaches, the patient's passive and dependent wishes are inevitably intensified and revived. The therapist, much as the good parent, remains available and supportive for the bereaved, even after the separation involved in growth has been accomplished. Termination is a form of mourning in which the therapist as a parent surrogate is renounced. To accomplish the work of the termination, the patient must have sufficient ego resources to tolerate the pain of loss and to undertake the work of mastery that is necessary for a developmental gain.

In terminating with persons who have previously had an abnormal reaction to loss of a significant person, the therapist must not push too rapidly toward termination, but allow much time for discussion, working through, reactions, acceptance, and more reactions, which should all be discussed at length. Termination is a two-way street. Lofgren has stated that termination should not occur until both the therapist and the patient agree simultaneously that the time has come and the separation has been appropriately mourned.[13]

REFERENCES

1. Glasser PH, Glasser LM: Families in Crisis. New York, Harper and Row, 1970, p 7
2. Hill R: Generic features of families under stress. *In* Parad HJ (ed): Crisis Intervention: Selected Readings. New York, Family Service Association of America, 1965, p 37
3. Hackett TP: Reorganizing and treating abnormal grief. Hosp Physician p:49–56, 1974
4. Deutsch H: Absence of grief. Psychoanal Q 6:12–22, 1937
5. Goldberg SB: Family tasks and reaction in the crisis of death. Soc Casework 54:398–405, 1973
6. Jackson DD, Bateson G: The question of family homeostasis. Psychiatr Q Suppl 31:79–90, 1957
7. Wynne LC, Rycoff IM, Day J, Hirsch SI: Pseudomutuality in family relationship of schizophrenia. Psychiatry 21:205–220, 1958

8. Ackerman N: Interlocking pathology in family relationships. *In* Rado S, Daniels G (eds): Changing Concepts of Psychoanalytic Medicine. New York, Grune & Stratton, 1956, pp 135–150
9. Owen M: A family concept of schizophrenia. *In* Jackson DD (ed): The Etiology of Schizophrenia. New York, Basic, 1960, pp 346–372
10. Satir V, Stachowiak J, Taschman HA: Helping Families to Change. New York, Aronson, 1975, p 112
11. Bell JE: Family Group Therapy. U.S. Public Health Monograph No. 64, Washington D.C., Government Printing Office, 1961
12. Minuchin S: Families and Family Therapy. Cambridge, Mass., Harvard University Press, 1974
13. Lofgren L: Personal communication. Los Angeles, Cal., 1975

PART V

Helping the Helpers: The Role of Liaison Psychiatry

Robert O. Pasnau
and Charles E. Hollingsworth

24

Mourning in the
Health Care Team

Over the years we have talked with many physicians, nurses, medical students, house officers, and social workers, and we have seen their families for help with their personal problems. For many reasons, some of them having to do with special reasons for the choice of the medical and nursing professions as a career, physicians and other health team members are especially vulnerable to loss and other emotional stresses. Vaillant and others have demonstrated some of the many ways that these stresses are handled by physicians.[1] In addition, the practice of the helping professions remains one of the most challenging and stressful occupations that an individual can undertake. It follows that assuming medical responsibility for and treating dying patients and bereaved families is one of the most prominent of these emotional stresses. This is evidenced by the depression and tension experienced by the staff of a dying or catastrophically ill person. The physician usually knows earlier than the patient that the illness is fatal. It drains him and affects his emotional state when he must convey this sad message to the patient and the patient's family. He may feel helpless in light of his awareness that the illness will be fatal, for it is a blow to his ego and feeling of effectiveness to know that the patient has a fatal disease and that death cannot be indefinitely delayed.

Facing a dying patient makes all members of the health care team aware of their own finiteness, and some are more susceptible than others to the depression this may arouse. This dying person may remind them of a close relative or friend who has died, and these associations often intensify the feelings of sadness, depression, and helplessness. The doctor's self-esteem is greatly affected by his ability to cure and bring relief. It is threatening to have to admit failure to a person whom he knows is depending on him. The doctor may consciously or unconsciously collude with the patient in denying or deceiving himself with regard to the impending death. Often the doctor rationalizes doing this because of his own need to be spared distress at the patient's dying. This distress may be less intense as the physician acquires more experience with dying patients, but even with more experience there are always some cases with which he becomes more emotionally involved than others.

It is important for the doctor, health care team, and patient to have hope and courage. Certainly medical miracles are part of the driving force behind desperate efforts to save the life of the terminally ill person. When the patient is suffering, in pain, the doctor and the caretakers also suffer. Most doctors try desperately to make the terminally ill comfortable. It is not necessary for a doctor to claim omnipotence to retain his patient's confidence, but he must have hope.

Honesty between doctor and patient is essential if confidence is to be maintained. "Many doctors are disinclined to speak freely with their patients, sparing in the information they divulge, but what they do tell their patients should always be in good faith."[2] The doctor should rarely make a deliberate statement to the patient to confirm the fatal nature of the illness. Often, however, this is inferred by chance or indirect remarks.[2]

Kubler-Ross, who has become renowned for her pioneering of interviews with seriously ill and dying patients, as well as for her research findings based on close association with hundreds of terminal patients, has written, "Never ever tell the patient he is dying. Never. I have never seen one case where this was helpful. When he is ready to talk about it—and if he has one single person who can listen—he will tell you. The listener must allow the patient to say it in his own way."[2] She has plotted the psychological states of many terminal patients, and she has described a pattern of the stages of dying. The physician's job, she believes, is to provide support and understanding, so that the patient can work through the normal stages of denial, anger, depression, and preparatory grief, to achieve a state of peaceful acceptance—not resignation—before death.

Sometimes the doctor's and health care team's uneasiness at the situation of working with a terminally ill patient and his/her family may lead them to avoid the patient, cut the visits short, or avoid mentioning any topic which could lead to making a choice between disquieting truth and lies. The doctor and health care team should continue to treat the adult patient as a mature person, capable of participating in discussions that affect him. It is all too easy to begin treating terminally ill patients as children.

The doctor and caring team must be aware that the dying patient and his family will employ many defense mechanisms in handling this stress. They may become preoccupied by some physical symptom or some relatively minor wrong, just as the physician and nurses may become excessively preoccupied with one medical problem that they can do something about, although they cannot change the course of the life-threatening illness. It is safer for the patient to displace his anxieties and preoccupations on to problems potentially less devastating than distress over his approaching death. The patient wants encouraging and reassuring remarks from his physician. The physician is caught in the bind of what to say and still be truthful.

There is good reason for the physician to be very cautious about ever telling a patient that he will not recover; some patients have reacted disastrously to finding out that they would never recover. The physician and health team are always seriously emotionally affected if their patient should take his own life. The physician and health care team most often feel the need to give the dying patient hope and encouragement; this can be emotionally draining if the terminal illness is prolonged, and if the physician has become emotionally involved with the patient's family in preparing them for accepting the inevitable death and laying the foundation for their appropriate grief and mourning. "Rightly or wrongly the physician may sense that his dying patient is criticising his effort, and this will further tempt him to avoid visits as far as he is able. A barrier of silence and unease can grow, untouched by the commonplaces that pass between them."[3]

Hinton has stated: "If the physician feels himself in harmony with the patient who is adapting to the progress of his disease, he will find that caring for the dying can be a rewarding experience rather than a confession of failure. He can use his medical knowledge and skill to prevent physical discomfort and so relieve his patient of one frequent cause of fear. The doctor will also note the comments of the dying person, listen sympathetically and learn to what extent his patient has gone towards accepting the end. He may need to do no more than listen or he may see that a little more help is needed. Understanding and intuition will guide when the need arises for encouragement, for reassurance over ill-founded fears, for changes of treatment, for help with the relatives, or for no more or less than human companionship."[3]

Kasper, in *The Meaning of Death*,[4] has indicated that the physician takes his own fears about death, puts them as intellectual questions, and tries to answer them for other people. If a physician has had a close call with a life-threatening illness as a child, it is likely to have influenced his decision to become a physician; in this way, he would be able to secure himself against the jeopardy of death, and would obtain dominion over his own anxiety by having the power to cure. One must not minimize the demands made on the physician and health care team members. Many physicians are in constant everyday contact with patients who arouse their own fears about dying and death, wound their narcissism, and impel them to prevent the impending situation. Ministry to the dying is extremely difficult if the physician himself is not quite reconciled to the idea of personal death.

Howell, who, as Professor and Chairman of Pediatrics at the University of California at San Diego, has seen more than 200 young patients die during her 20 years as a pediatric hematologist, continues to stress the doctor's responsibility both to the child and to the parents. The physician's work is still unfinished when death occurs—the family must be salvaged and restored.[2] In order to do this work, the physician must himself be healed.

Schools of nursing, more so than medical schools, include in their curricula some consideration of the nurse's responsibility toward the dying patient and the relatives who attend him. Almost all schools help prepare their nurses to understand the patient's emotional response to dying, his uses of denial and the process of separation, anticipating grief of family members, and emotional reactions of the hospital staff. Student nurses also have classroom discussions on the controversial subjects of euthanasia, transplantation, and the definitions of death. Most nursing schools are continuing to update their curricula to include more coverage of the care of the dying patient and his family.

In general, medical schools, social work training programs, and psychiatry residency training programs need much revision of their curricula to include and expand programs on dying, grief, mourning, bereavement, readjustment, and resolution.

Liaison psychiatry has taken upon itself the role of helping the helpers. Sometimes, when the stresses become too great, individual counseling or therapy for the health team member may be required. It is usually not advisable for the liaison psychiatrist to provide this counseling himself on any long-term basis, but he is obviously the psychiatrist to whom the team member should turn initially for evaluation and advice. Often, however, help and support are available from the group, through special programs, discussions, and rounds. Some of these programs are discussed in the following chapters. It is urged that some group activity be provided to the health care team of every facility responsible for the care of dying people and their families.

REFERENCES

1. Vaillant GE, Sobowall NC, McArthur C: Stress handled by physicians: some psychologic vulnerabilities of physicians. N Engl J Med 287:372–375, 1972
2. Fishbein M(ed): Dealing with Death. Med World News 12(20):35, 1971
3. Hinton J: The dying and the doctor. *In* Toynbee A(ed): Man's Concern with Death. New York, McGraw–Hill, 1968, p 43
4. Kasper S: The doctor and death. *In* Feifel H(ed): The Meaning of Death. New York, McGraw–Hill, 1959, pp 259–270

Cathie-Ann Lippman
and Ken Carlson

25

A Model Liaison Program for the Obstetrics Staff: Workshop on the Tragic Birth

Childbirth can be either a joyous, rewarding, and overwhelmingly happy occasion, or it can be a tragic and emotionally devastating experience. In the first case, there is the delivery of a well-formed and healthy infant; in the latter case there is the delivery of a stillborn, malformed, or distressed infant, or injury to the mother. According to the literature and the authors' own experience at a large university teaching hospital, a tragic birth occurs approximately 6–8 percent of the time.[12] In a hospital where 200–250 births take place each month, there are 12–20 such incidents, or 144–240 a year. Yet little teaching concerning the psychological impact of these incidents is pursued in medical or nursing school curriculums.

In these cases, the psychological impact on the parents arises primarily from the loss of an expectation, which most often manifests itself as an acute grief reaction with mourning. However, parents have reacted with severe depression, reactive psychoses, and physical difficulties related to the current stresses. In this regard, the psychological care which the obstetrics staff must provide these patients is of primary importance.

The consequences of a "tragic" birth often reach beyond the parents and infant to affect the entire hospital staff dealing with the situation. Anxiety, helplessness, and depression are inherent in the process of caring for these patients and their families. The staff is often not aware of this source of frustration, and do not have the knowledge or the organizational flexibility to deal with these patients adequately.

In our hospital, the chief of obstetrical anesthesiology was one of the first of those who recognized the needs for the staff for special training in such situations. Consequently, he initiated the request to the psychiatric consultation liaison team. As the liaison group began to develop a training program, they became more fully appreciative of the emotional impact of this experience for both patient and staff, and impressed at the complex organizational and social situations these problems create. As a result, they began to observe these patients systematically during the delivery process and on the floor, discuss their care with staff, and review the available literature dealing with the phenomenon of the "tragic" birth. The end product was a four-hour workshop, presented to the physicians and staff of the delivery room, obstetrical ward, and neonatal nursery. With each presentation of the workshop, more confirmatory feedback comments were gathered from the audiences.

This chapter presents a synopsis of the workshop. It represents the distillation of numerous comments, literature review, and hours of contact with patients and staff caring for the patients who have experienced a "tragic" birth. The goal of the workshop was to help the staff deal with the families who experienced traumatic births in a way that was comfortable for them and would have the best long-range psychological effect for both parents. To do this, the content of the workshop was divided into five areas.

SYSTEMS FORMULATION

The systems model represents pictorially a concept of the processes involved in the different types of problem births (Figure 25-1). Throughout the system runs the general theme that the experience of a traumatic birth involves the loss of a happy expectation and substitution of the experience of death, the threat of death, or living with a defective child. Even before the woman enters the hospital, there are factors that affect the mother and the family and which will subsequently affect the staff and their interaction with the family. Prior to hospitalization, the mother's attitudes toward herself, the pregnancy, and the role of the baby are influenced by family relations, expectations she has developed from familial, societal, and cultural attitudes,

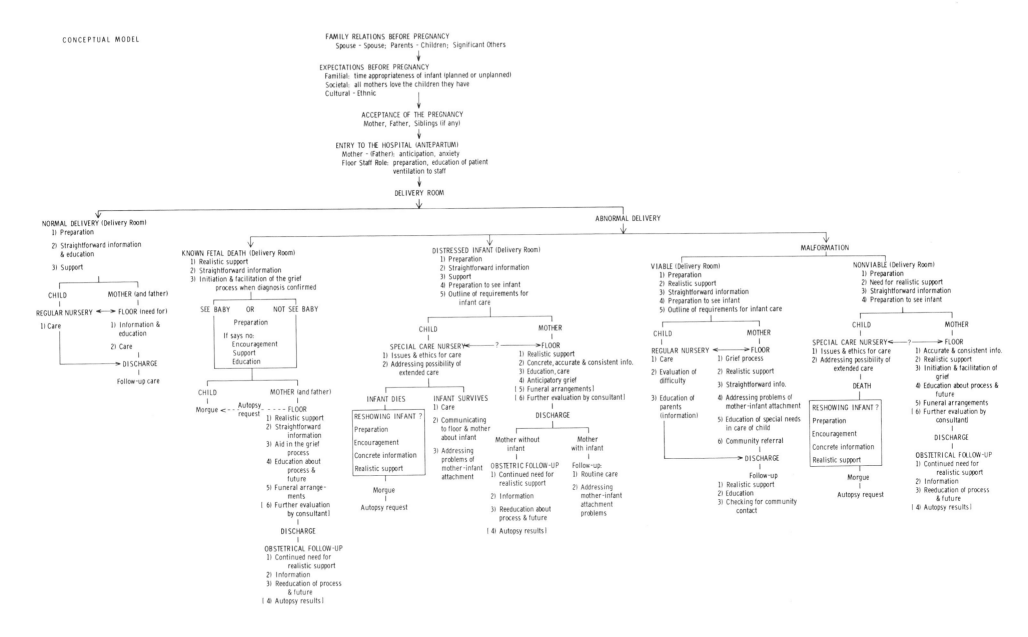

Figure 25-1. A conceptual model of the processes involved in different types of problem births.

and the acceptance of the pregnancy by significant members of the family and close friends. For example, whether or not the baby was planned or unplanned, or how the pregnancy conformed to the mother's moral attitudes or the family's financial status, are important considerations. Whether or not the pregnancy might jeopardize the mother's health, whether or not she has a chronic illness, or whether or not as a result of the pregnancy and delivery her physical status is threatened and her body left irreversibly damaged, are also important. These (and many other) factors accompany the mother and family when they are greeted by the hospital staff at admission.

It is the staff's responsibility to help the mother prepare for delivery by educating her about hospital procedure, the anticipated delivery, and what the staff expects of her. She should be allowed to ventilate her fears and worries freely and completely. This also includes giving support to the rest of the family and helping them in a similar fashion.

The model describes the progress from the delivery room to discharge. There are two types of deliveries. The most frequent is the normal delivery with the uncomplicated arrival of a healthy infant. The abnormal delivery includes known fetal death, the distressed infant, and the malformed infant. Despite this diversity in types of births, there are themes common to all. It is important and helpful for the staff to recognize these in order to provide the maximum care. What the model helps to demonstrate is the need for teamwork, such as close collaboration among all the services and disciplines to ensure communication of current and accurate information to each staff person, and thus to the mother and family. The increasing complexity in these processes becomes obvious as the different problem births are studied. Hence, the work of the staff becomes more complicated and the patient's experience more difficult. For that reason, extra psychological care must be available for the patient.

The process of the normal delivery is relatively straightforward. The mother requires preparation, straightforward information, and education, and support in the delivery room, on the floor, and at follow-up. When the delivery is abnormal, the mother requires further help, and psychological care has to be magnified considerably.

In the case of the known fetal death, the mother will maintain some hope for the delivery of a normal, healthy infant, despite the certainty of the diagnosis. Often she will not believe otherwise until the dead baby is born. Whether or not the mother should see the baby is one of the major problems in the delivery room. Except in the rarest instances, when there is no resemblance to a human form, the mother should see her baby. If she is hesitant, the staff will need to inform her of the importance of this and support her in the process. They should also prepare her to meet new people, including personnel from the Office of Decedent Affairs, pathology department, and often from the funeral home. The floor nurses and physicians should support the mother and father in the grief process, in addition to providing the standard care required.

The same issues of viewing the infant and interaction with other personnel arise in the instances of birth of a distressed or malformed infant. The situation becomes much more complex, because more uncertainty is introduced. The distressed infant may live or die. The extra demands on the staff include allowing and helping the mother to grieve while monitoring her responses, not allowing anticipatory grief to go so far that the mother prematurely believes the baby is dead. With delivery of the malformed but viable infant, the staff needs to recognize that, although the mother has a live baby, she grieves at the loss of the normal infant she expected. The malformed, nonviable, but not yet dead infant's delivery combines all the features of the previous cases. Thus with any of these complicated deliveries the mother will require additional education, straightforward information and additional psychosocial support by the staff. Follow-up care of the mother, the family, and, in appropriate cases, the infant, also demands the extra attention.

LITERATURE REVIEW

The amount of literature relating to these difficult deliveries is increasing rapidly. The articles may be divided into three major categories: The first reports research studies of the parent(s) experiences in these specific instances and evaluation of care techniques. The second category describes the process experienced by the patient and, based on this, gives suggestions for intervention by the staff. The third is made up of anecdotal reports.

Research studies have tended to look at the response of the mother under the various circumstances. These include the reactions to premature birth seen as an acute emotional disorder,[3] the emotional reaction to a stillbirth[1,2] the parents' adaptation to the birth of a malformed infant,[4,5] and the response to transfer of the infant to a referral center for intensive care.[6,7] In contrast to organized empirical studies, much of the literature describes the process of the parental experience, and often makes suggestions as to how the staff might intervene. These papers describe the normal response, abnormal response, the survivor syndrome, and anticipatory grief. They discuss reactions to a stillbirth of the family and the physician,[8-10] or the response to the birth of a defective child.[11,12] Others, in addition to describing the normal grief process, tell the staff how to work with the patients.[13-17] Many articles make reference to Lindemann for his evaluation of the normal and pathologic grief process and the survivor syndrome.[18] Few, however, discuss the issue of anticipatory grief in its relation to these problem births. There are general articles in this area that provide an approach to this aspect of the process.[19-22]

Many articles in the third category are personal anecdotes often written by nurses who themselves underwent a traumatic delivery. Their moving descriptions cover all aspects; e.g., the birth of a premature infant,[23] a deformed infant[15,24,25]; or a stillbirth.[7,26-28]

Throughout the literature is the pervasive theme of loss, of feeling devastated, and of the need to find the means to meet and overcome these traumatic experiences.

THE GRIEF PROCESS

Patients and their families who have experienced a tragic birth experience an acute grief reaction. It appears that the period of mourning which these patients experience has much in common with other descriptions of a grief process.[14,17,27-29] Because it also has certain unique components, it is necessary to revise certain notions about this grief process.

The grief reaction that these patients experience is dominated by the loss of an expectation. Partially, what seems to be mourned is the lack of a joyous event, for which two adults, their significant friends and relatives, and society has prepared them during the previous 7–9 months. When the tragic event occurs, the infant's mother and father respond initially with shock and disbelief. The reality of the event which has already taken place is undeniable. It seems that the mother begins to feel guilt and shame. Somehow, the tragic event is interpreted as a statement of the mother's own personal self-esteem. Simultaneously, the father begins to express anger and anxiety. Although both parents, at this point, express themselves differently, careful interrogation reveals that they are both responding to an overwhelming feeling of loss. They may then, particularly the mother, experience a feeling of helplessness accompanied by rage, which is often diffuse and intense. During this period, the mother appears markedly depressed.

The rage often resolves into a period of blame and bitterness. There is noted ambivalency during this time, with blame directed at both herself and others. This is likely an attempt at restitution or bargaining.[29] Finally, both parents reach a period of resolution and acceptance of the tragic event. During this time there is a period of acquiescence in the event and planning for the future. It is here, however, that misguided "simple solutions" to the tragic event can take place.[10,14] Among the "solutions" that have the severest consequences are a mother asking for a tubal ligation or a father requesting a vasectomy in order that this experience may never happen again. Other simple solutions include replacing the loss of an expectation with a pet, development of new hobbies, or adoption of a new life style. The important therapeutic consideration here is that the long-range effect of these simple solutions can be more devastating than the original trauma and grief related to the loss. It is important to alert the mother and father to these possibilities.

The theme of a loss of an expectation was prominent in presenting the grief process just outlined, primarily for developing "process comments" that could be used by staff members when dealing with these patients. Secondarily, it was developed to alert the patient to these time-limited processes.

It must be emphasized that the above discussion is an outline. This model does not imply that this is *all* a patient experiences, or that it is always experienced in the ordered fashion in which it is presented.

COMMUNICATION METHODS

For purposes of teaching and training for interventions, the notion of communication was used to discuss approaches for patients who have lost an "expected" infant, and brief therapy techniques. As an anchor for all communication models, the concept of providing "realistic support" was introduced.[14] This is defined as a period of time when the staff person can purposely encourage the mother (father, family member) to express herself (himself) concerning the loss of the expected infant, and to do this when the staff person can listen patiently without having to "do something." The intention of such support is to create an atmosphere where open communication is possible in a tension-filled situation. The mother, father, or other family members should feel free to express feelings, cry, remain silent, talk, or receive information. This is a rather simple concept that most mental health professionals accept on face value. However, when dealing with medical personnel who are accustomed to providing "tangible" care (e.g., drawing blood, taking temperatures, recording blood pressures, etc.), the concept of realistic support may seem a stagnant activity. This issue, therefore, assumes prominent teaching importance.

Several formulations of communication were introduced and discussed simultaneously with explanations and examples of brief psychotherapy techniques.[30] The procedures described, first, how to ask non-demand, open-ended questions, e.g., "This has been a difficult time for you, are you ready to talk?" The nature of advice-giving as a communication was also discussed. Self-disclosure, its reciprocal nature, and its use in facilitating discussion in a tension-filled situation was also a focus in teaching. The value and technique of making reflective comments, confirmatory statements, and comments concerning grief process were introduced. The efficacy and timing of giving straightforward information as a therapeutic tool was also described. Finally, therapeutic use of silences and nonverbal communications were presented.

In order to illustrate pragmatically the models of communication and therapy techniques, a brief "listening" workshop requiring audience participation was included. At this time, examples titled "How We Cut People Off" were gone over in detail. The purpose of this was to exemplify common pitfalls when attempting to facilitate another person's expression of feeling.

All examples and discussions of techniques included a heavy emphasis on the interpersonal nature of psychological care. A particular effort was made to avoid mechanization of this care. Each person was encouraged to use the principles taught as guidelines rather than as dogma dictation in their interventions. This provided the mother and father with the opportunity for catharsis and integration rather than denial of the experience of a tragic birth.

It was also necessary to address the role of empathy in the therapeutic intervention. When caring for a person in a physical way who has just experienced a trauma, empathy by staff members plays some role for most individuals.[7,9,17,27] Therefore, a brief discussion was held of how empathy is helpful in setting an atmosphere for permitting feelings instead of not allowing them. Empathy that can sometimes be harmful, including overidentification and/or premature reassurance, was discussed.

SUGGESTIONS FOR INTERVENTION

The end result of this work was a list of general rules or guiding principles for providing psychological care to the mothers and fathers who experience a tragic birth. These principles include special suggestions for dealing with them when in the delivery room and on the obstetrical floor.

The first general principle is the importance of human contact. Often it is assumed that these patients want to be alone. The patient, in turn, interprets this as avoidance and that others consider her to be fully accountable for the incident, hence "undesireable" as a person. The purpose of this principle is to help the staff appreciate that their presence alone can help these mothers and fathers recognize that they are worthwhile as individuals.

The second, and perhaps most important, principle is not to isolate the mother or father from the process that occurs when a tragic birth takes place. The purpose of this is to help restore the personal integrity that the parents brought with them to the hospital. The simple way to follow this suggestion is to give the mother and father some control over daily routine by having them make choices and emphasizing their ability to do so. Choices that these individuals can make should concern such things as their room,[10] roommate or no roommate, and analgesic medication. Likewise, in discussions with them, all volitional aspects of their behavior can be subtly reinforced. Such comments as "Tell me what has happened since you *decided* to become a parent" will aim toward the goal of this suggestion. It is important to remember that as part of the process in any tragic birth, there are two individuals who have considered themselves parents for the past 7–9 months. Both appreciate being recognized as such.[15]

The third principle is that these individuals receive factual, updated, and straightforward information concerning their own condition and that of the infant, if it is living. This requires a coordinated effort of delivery room, and obstetrical and neonatal nursery personnel. It is of primary importance that all personnel dealing with the patient and her family be privy to and share the same information. Psychological trauma for a patient and family frequently occurs when contradictory information is shared with them by individuals acting in a mutually exclusive manner, even though they are caring for the same patient.

The final general principle proposed was borrowed from Seitz and Warrick.[14] This principle states that the amount of support a patient needs will be inversely proportional to the support that she gets from her husband and family. This is an important principle that has two ammended cautions. First, the family (particularly fathers) also grieve the loss that has just occurred. They, too, may need similar staff interventions that are recommended for the patient. Therefore, whenever possible it is encouraged that the staff member meet with the patient and her family together. Second, it is very important to note whether the family is inhibiting the grief process of the mother. The long-range impact of inhibiting the grief process can be destructive.[18] If this is occurring, it is recommended that this be openly discussed with the family. In order to assess this situation, there should be a minimum of two prolonged contacts with the patient (mother) by the floor nurse and primary physician.

Delivery Room

When a tragic birth occurs, it is important to realize that the mother has just experienced the physical stress of active labor, and must simultaneously face the emotional trauma of a loss. The delivery room staff likewise have faced the physical stresses of delivery, and must simultaneously deal with their own high level of anxiety in a situation that quickly becomes tension-filled. This set of circumstances creates an extremely difficult atmosphere in which to function. However, what is done and said to a mother and/or father in the delivery room can be of significant psychological importance.

The loss of what is expected is undeniable in the delivery room. The long awaited cry of a new infant may not occur, the viewing of a healthy, well formed infant may quickly be shattered, or the news that the infant is in good health is not heard. In any of these cases, the mother and father begin to grieve. The implicit goal in the recommended interventions for the delivery room personnel is to help initiate and facilitate this grief reaction.

As with all patients, there is a need to emphasize the maintenance of a positive direction of the delivery. Whether the staff suspects a stillbirth or malformed infant, the mother usually maintains her expectation for the delivery of a healthy, well-formed infant. It is the staff's role to emphasize the importance of a smooth delivery, soliciting the patient's help, without emphasizing her own health, which, this time, may later cause the mother to "magically" believe that she somehow sacrificed the infant to make herself more comfortable. A simple comment like "We know this is a difficult time for you, but it is important you decide to help us with the delivery" will often solicit the woman's cooperation in a warm and empathetic way, while making her part of the process.

When a tragic birth occurs, it is of primary importance that the diagnosis be established as soon as possible. This is in the delivery room. Both the mother and father need concrete, accurate information as best as it can be supplied at this time. This information must come from the physician. It will need to be repeated several times before she leaves the hospital. Simple, straightforward comments by the obstetrician and/or pediatrician, like "Your baby is small and has an atypical heart beat; that is all we can tell you now, we need to do further diagnostic work; we will get back to you; as soon as we know something more we will tell you," or "Your son (daughter) has what is called a cleft palate . . . " can serve this purpose.

Following such a tragic birth, it is important for the delivery room staff to recognize how difficult this process is for the mother and father. The staff should allow and encourage the parents to express their feelings while still in the delivery room. As mentioned earlier, it is desirable that the infant be shown to the parents, unless extreme circumstances prevail.

While in the delivery room, one individual should establish personal contact with the patient. This person can provide information and take responsibility for lessening the "deadly silence" that often occurs when a tragic birth takes place.[14] This is extremely important, because should the mother become detached (e.g., hallucinating or delerious), this person can assume responsibility for taking charge of and reorienting her. These patients should never be left alone.

Obstetrical Ward

Many of the suggestions that encompassed floor care were articulated earlier in the teaching concerning communication and brief therapy techniques. However, when feasible, it seems important that *one* floor nurse from each shift be assigned to each of these patients consistently during the patient's hospital stay. This nurse is responsible for the care and emotional support, and being a focal point for coordinating information imparted to the patient. Whenever possible, the patient's antepartum nurse, if willing, should be the patient's postpartum nurse.

While on the obstetrical service, it is also the responsibility of the floor nurses to validate the experience of the mother and father, create an atmosphere in which open communication is possible, and provide the patient with appropriate education. This education can center around the grief process outlined earlier, and, when applicable, around the care of an infant with special problems, whatever those problems may be.

The final recommendation for obstetrical service personnel is to make themselves available to the patient. There should be regularly scheduled, intermittent visits to the patient, as well as other brief, randomized periods of contact. During this time, both the patient's physical and psychological needs can be cared for. In this regard, it is important that a caretaker unobtrusively announce the dual purpose to the mother and father with a simple comment like "I am here to take your vital signs and spend minutes with you." By allotting specific time, the mother and father can titrate their disclosure of feeling or questioning, and the nurse can regulate her communications or therapeutic interventions.

Conclusion

Childbirth can be a devastating psychological experience when there is a stillbirth or the birth of a malformed, very sick, or nonviable infant. The psychological care of the families assumes primary importance in their health maintenance. The responsibility for this care routinely falls to the hospital staff, who, sometimes because of a lack of experience, feelings of helplessness or anxiety, find this task most difficult. Suggestions for dealing with these families in mourning have been presented.

REFERENCES

1. Cullberg J: Mental reactions of women to perinatal death. *In* Karger B(ed): Psychosomatic Medicine in Obstetrics and Gynecology. London, Karger, 1972, pp 326–329
2. Wolff JR, Nielson PE, Schiller P: The emotional reaction to a stillbirth. Am J of Obstetr Gynecol 108:73–79, 1970
3. Kaplan DM, Mason EA: Maternal reactions to premature birth viewed as an acute emotional disorder. Am J Orthopsychiatry 30:539–552, 1960
4. Protar D, Baskiewicz BA, Irvin N, Kennell J, Klaus M: The adaptation of parents to the birth of an infant with a congenital malformation: a hypothetical model. Pediatrics 56:710–717, 1975
5. Mercer AT: Mothers' responses to their infants with defects. Nurs Res 23:133–137, 1974
6. Benfield GD, Leib SA, Reuter J: Grief response of patients after referral of the critically ill newborn to a regional center. N Engl J Med 294:975–978, 1976
7. Penfold KM: Supporting motherlove. Am J Nurs 74:464–467, 1974
8. Bourne S: The psychological effects of stillbirth on the doctor. *In* Karger B(ed): Psychosomatic Medicine in Obstetrics and Gynecology. London, Karger, 1972, pp 333–334
9. Lewis E: Reactions to stillbirth. *In* Karger B(ed): Psychosomatic Medicine in Obstetrics and Gynecology. London, Karger, 1972, pp 323–325

10. Wolff JR: The emotional reaction to a stillbirth. *In* Karger B (ed): Psychosomatic Medicine in Obstetrics and Gynecology. London, Karger, 1972, pp 330–332
11. Rafalovich S: The relationship of parents after the birth of a child with a congenital defect. Reconstr Surg Traumatics 14:154–156, 1974
12. Solnit AI, Stark MH: Mourning and the birth of a defective child. Psychoanal Stud Child 16:523–537, 1961
13. Carr EF, Oppe TE: The birth of an abnormal child: telling the parents. Lancet 2(7733): 1075–1077, 1971
14. Seitz PM, Warrick LH: Perinatal death and the grieving mother. Am J Nurs 74:2028–2033, 1974
15. Stanko B: Crisis intervention after the birth of a defective child. Can Nurse 69:27–28, 1973
16. Yates SA: Stillbirth: what a staff can do. Am J Nurs 72:1592–1594, 1972
17. Zahourek R, Jensen JS: Grieving and the loss of the newborn. Am J Nurs 73:836–839, 1973
18. Lindemann E: Symptomatology and management of acute grief. Am J Psychiatry 101:141–148, 1944
19. Blank RH: Anticipatory grief and mourning. *In* Schoenberg B et al. (eds): Anticipatory Grief. Columbia Univ. Press, 1974, pp 276–279
20. Nighswonger CA: Vectors and vital signs in grief synchronization. In Schoenberg, B. et al. (eds): Anticipatory Grief. New York, Columbia Univ. Press, 1974, pp 267–275
21. Reeves RB: Reflections on two false expectations. *In* Schoenberg, B et al. (eds): Anticipatory Grief. New York, Columbia University Press, 1974, pp 281–284
22. Rinear EE: Helping the survivors of expected death. Nursing 5:60–65, 1975
23. Goodman MB: Two mothers' reactions to the deaths of their premature infants. JOGN Nurs 4 (May–June): 25–27, 1975
24. Anonymous: Personal Paper: Having a congenitally deformed baby. Lancet 1(7718): 1499–1501, 1973
25. Young I: A mother's grief work following the death of her deformed child. Matern Child Nurs 4:57–62, 1975
26. Johnson JM: Stillbirth—a personal experience. Am J Nurs 72:1595–1596, 1972
27. Klopf SK: Please don't go away: a crisis when nobody intervened. Nurs Clin North Am 9:77–80, 1974
28. Mooney B: A stillbirth: from agony to acceptance. *Los Angeles Times*, February 8, 1976, Sec. 3, pp 1, 4
29. Kubler-Ross E: On Death and Dying. New York, Macmillan, 1969
30. Kardener SH: A methodologic approach to crisis therapy. Am J Psychother 29:4–13, 1975

Fawzy I. Fawzy,
David Wellisch,
and Joel Yager

26

Psychiatric Liaison to the Bone-Marrow Transplant Project

Bone-marrow transplantation is an experimental procedure for the treatment of leukemias and aplastic anemias that are unresponsive to conventional therapies. The procedure requires patients to be pre-treated with massive doses of radiotherapy and chemotherapy to sup-press their immune systems, following which they receive intravenous infusions of marrow that has been surgically removed from an antigen-ically compatible blood relative. Patients must then remain in reverse isolation for a three-week period because of their extreme susceptibil-ity to infection, and during this time the marrow graft either succeeds or fails. Although marrow transplantation is a procedure of last resort, the attendant morbidity and mortality is considerable. While it is diffi-cult to attribute these occurrences to the procedure rather than to the ongoing illness, some staff have the impression that the procedure often increases the patients' discomfort and occasionally hastens their demise.

Psychiatric intervention is necessary at several levels. In addition to having to deal with frequent deaths among patients in whom consid-erable attention and effort have been invested (as occurs in any oncol-ogy unit), the professional staff must cope individually and collectively with their ambivalent attitudes regarding the value and harm of the procedure. Their participation in the project, the quality of care they can render, and the nature of the information about the procedure they provide to patients and relatives are immediately related to how they deal with these conflicted issues, both personally and as a coordinated staff. Patients and their families require assistance in their efforts to intellectually and emotionally appreciate information offered to them by way of "informed consent" procedures, and also in their efforts to grapple with the general problems of life-threatening illness. The radiotherapy, chemotherapy, and isolation requirements of the procedure itself contribute to the likelihood of psychiatric complications in patients.

In response to a clearly perceived need for psychiatric consultation to this project, a three-tiered program of psychosocial care was instituted through the Psychiatric Consultation–Liaison Service. This program, now in its third year, focuses on helping the medical team helping the patient, and helping the families.

HELPING THE MEDICAL TEAM

In recent years, numbers of clinical research centers have been established in which selected patient populations are gathered for the dual goal of medical research and patient care. It is recognized that these hospital subcultures clearly represent a departure from traditional medical or surgical-ward settings in the kinds of human issues, values, and attitudes prevailing in the care of the seriously ill.

Nurses are trained in the care of the ill with the expectation that in an atmosphere of cooperative, diligent care, patients will, in a fair percentage of cases, either be cured or improved to a significant and lasting degree. Clearly, this is not the case in the bone-marrow transplant unit. The nurse is left with ambivalent feelings about being there. Most nurses have a sense of professional obligation to spend some part of their nursing careers taking care of the most difficult problems. However, striking changes in the perceived role of nurses on the bone-marrow transplant unit make it difficult for them to continue to have this feeling of obligation. Many, early in their experience, say that they have paid "the debt" and will probably quit a unit in which the patients never get well.

There is an additional problem for the staff of a research unit. Because of the relative lack of knowledge about the significance of the research among the nurses, an atmosphere develops in which some nurses feel that things are being done *to* the patients rather than *for* them. There are very few and infrequent attempts to orient the staff about the significance of the research and also to give them follow-up information about discharged patients or families. Deprived on the one hand of some of the satisfactions of professional competency through patient response, and on the other of the intellectual justification and research rationalization available to the doctors, their professional identity is jeopardized.

Sometimes there are disguised outbursts of anger at physicians for poor outcomes. More commonly this anger is displaced to other nurses and paramedical staff (e.g., social workers and dieticians), resulting in an increase in tension in the ward.

On admission to the bone-marrow transplant unit, a tacit agreement is struck between the nurses and the patient. The patient contributes his physical being and his cooperation in a joint research and, hopefully, a therapeutic endeavor. To the greatest possible extent the staff contributes to the welfare of the patient. In instances when things go badly for a patient, staff anxiety mounts. Nurses may frankly express feelings of guilt for not having kept up their part of the bargain. On occasions, guilt and anxiety in the ward staff is so high it has paralyzing effects.

Residents and interns have very bad feelings about working on this unit. Except for emergencies, only routine decisions concerning patient care are made by the ward resident/intern. For some residents, the restrictions on overall responsibility contribute to reduce motivation to wrestle with the psychological problems of the patients; others resent those restrictions. Some count the days remaining until his or her responsibility ends. Some can take refuge in the intellectual research aspects of the case, no matter how grim the patient's situation becomes. Some use the nurses and ward personnel as a buffer between them and exposure to patients. Their identities as physicians, the research goals, and the time-limited rotation on the unit form natural points of conflict with the nursing and paramedical staff, whose priorities center on patient care and whose time commitment to the unit is indefinite.

In order to deal with some of these staff problems, the liaison group first identified the process and the problems, and set up regular group meetings. Although there was some initial resistance on the parts of some of the physicians, gradually all concerned began to attend regularly. Feelings were explored, communication avenues opened up, and the special problems of working in this type of environment were discussed.

As a result, nursing absenteeism and transfer declined sharply, house-staff began spending more time on the unit, and patient morale was noted to improve. However, the feelings of loss and mourning continued to be very painful areas which required ongoing work as the project entered its third year.

HELPING THE PATIENTS

Patients with life-threatening illnesses carry their premorbid personality structures into the illness complete with their characteristic and usual strengths, adaptive features, and coping mechanisms, as well as with their characteristic neuroses, character defects, and decompensatory reactions in the face of stresses. All patients with life-threatening illnesses must learn to live in their "limbo state" and to marshall their defenses to deal with the massive and covertly ever-present anxiety inherent in such a condition. We have found that all patients with a life-threatening illness are frequently pushed by the illness, and existential concerns surrounding the illness, into very extreme expressions of their personality configurations. For example, a person who is characteristically obsessive–compulsive might become extremely rigid, structured, and questioning of each procedure in the face of a terminal illness.

For the bone-marrow transplant patient, who also has coped with a life-threatening illness for a lengthy time period before entering the Bone Marrow Transplant program, there are additional stresses. Inherent in the psychosocial adaptation to the bone-marrow transplant situation is coping with sensory deprivation due to the lengthy reverse-isolation, and adjustment to the overwhelming dependency on the bone-marrow transplant unit nurses. As noted before, personality style interacts significantly with degree and style of adaptation to both isolation and dependency. Some patients become overwhelmingly dependent, regressed, and unable to deal with the isolation without significant anxiety. Others at the opposite extreme reject dependency on nurses and choose to remain as isolated as possible.

In general, we have found a three-stage developmental pattern of psychosocial adaptation to the bone-marrow transplant. Stage one begins with introduction into the program and is characterized by "aggressive optimism" as the central psychological feature, with formation of a working alliance with the physicians and especially the nurses. From a psychiatric standpoint, this is the stage of transference formation with the physician and nurse "parental figures." These transference reactions range from neurotic and nonadaptive to positive and functional. The task of the liaison consultant is to maximize a positive working alliance during this first stage.

Of the various factors that tend to contribute to the patient's and their families' discontent, certainly one of the most important is poor communication between doctor and patient. In modern medical practice, which is now focused predominantly on technical knowledge, the physician may be engrossed in technical concerns and scientific technology that mystify the patient. The legal requirements of "informed consent" mean that the patient should be made aware of "The nature, duration, and purpose of the experiment; the method and means by which it is to be conducted; all inconveniences and hazards reasonably to be expected; and the effects upon his health or his person which may possibly come from his participation in the experiment." Yet, as Alsobrook has stated, "There are no practical guidelines as to how far a physician should go in explaining the risks in order to obtain informed consent."[1] A further complication is that under stress patients may understand very little of what the physician is saying and may not truly be capable of informed consent. The task of the liaison psychiatrist is to help the physician learn more effective ways of keeping communication with his patients open.

Stage one ends with the full body radiation and transfusion of bone marrow from the matched donor. Psychologically, it terminates with the advent of the massive physical sequelae resulting from the sub-lethal doses of cytoxan combined with the full body radiation, which catapults the patient into an ultra-dependent relationship with the nursing team. Stage two is characterized by the patient's physical illness. Intervention by the mental health team is rarely required by the patient. This is the stage in which a great deal of time must be spent with nursing personnel, as they spend what seems to them to be endless hours in isolation with these severely ill patients. They begin to feel ignored, isolated, and deprived themselves.

Stage three begins when and *if* the physical sequelae of this procedure begin to remit and the patient begins to have the dawning awareness that he or she will leave both the "protective cocoon" of the isolation room and of the larger hospital ward. Frustration, anger, and impatience are the most frequent psychological features of this stage. It is not unusual for the patient to angrily confront staff and family with the statement, "If I had known that it would be this bad and that I'd feel like this I would never have done this." This rather understandable feeling is met with enormous desperation and resistance by family and hospital staff alike. The patient frequently and angrily resists taking oral medications. It becomes apparent that these patients have experienced repeated, traumatic, and overwhelming assaults on their body boundaries, which in this stage are no longer interpreted as being helpful by the patient and are defended against. They cannot wait to leave the isolation room in this stage. When actually presented with this possibility they are often fearful about leaving the room and do not do so unless strongly urged. Stage three ends when the patient leaves the hospital.

We believe that each bone-marrow transplant patient requires an in-depth psychological and psychiatric assessment prior to his admission to the unit, and individual psychotherapy by a mental health professional during his hospitalization. The authors are in the midst of a project designed to test this assumption using a controlled experimental approach. However, in our experience, the usual psychiatric consultation approach "as needed" is not really sufficient for these patients.

The psychosocial stresses of the illness and procedure are by no means terminated with discharge from hospitalization, and often further psychiatric assistance is required on an outpatient basis.

HELPING THE FAMILIES

The emotional stresses and psychic exhaustion which characterize the psychological situation of the bone-marrow transplant patient are also clearly reflected in the patient's family. We have not observed any family which did not have very strong affectional experience as a result of participation in this procedure. This is not to say that all families integrate such powerful affects with equal psychological agility or reflect the same coping styles. In fact, we have observed coping styles across a wide spectrum.

The families of bone-marrow transplant patients have additional problems above and beyond those which are usual for families of cancer patients, as previously described by Kubler-Ross,[2] Weisman,[3] and others. These families have gone through the emotional struggles and adjustments that accompany living with a family member who has a terminal disease in the "end stage" which has either not responded or ceased to respond to treatment. With the possibility of bone-marrow transplantation, the family once again takes a ride on an "emotional roller-coaster," reversing the psychological steps that have been taken. They are now asked to return to optimism and hope.

The group of patients usually recommended and accepted for this rigorous, exhausting, and depleting procedure are generally younger than most cancer patients. It is never easy to adjust to cancer and patient terminality in a family member, but to adjust to it in a child, a teen-ager, or a young adult in his or her twenties presents fearsome difficulties. We have seen families recreate their emotional journeys across the steps of adjustment to the disease in a compacted amount of time, but this time with diminished resources emotionally. This depleted emotional state is often obscured by a thin defense of very unrealistic optimism, and thus is not obvious to the staff or physician.

The displacement of these families from their normal environs and usual support systems of families and friends is another seriously complicating factor. With the growth of our program's reputation, we have had families come from all over the U.S.A. as well as from other countries as far away as Australia. This added factor has further imbalanced family homeostasis and forced them into a state of massive emotional disequilibrium. An example was a working class family from a midwestern state who arrived with three children, including the ill-patient daughter. The father had abandoned his job. The mother was in a state of extreme emotional exhaustion. The father's presence was unique in that his job as a long-distance truck driver was characterized by his not spending much time with his family. This hospitalization forced the mother and father into an intimacy and joint decision-making position that neither was familiar with nor would tolerate. Old marital troubles errupted. The ill daughter felt responsible and attempted vainly to counsel the parents.

The economic disruption of the families has usually reached a peak by the time the patients are candidates for bone-marrow transplantation. The families usually repress this anxiety. In fact, the usual family coping mechanism at the beginning of bone-marrow transplantation is massive repression and a resulting high optimism. Their behavior is characterized by an overriding tension and tenuousness which serves to maintain the energy devoted to the denial, repression, and optimism. The liaison consultant is faced with a very special therapeutic problem. This is not a time for uncovering work or basic structural changes in these families. He must make a quick but accurate assessment of the family systems and work from a position of rapid, short-term interventions which enhance defenses and do not shift the balance toward a more negative direction. He should adopt the strategy of showing up defenses, patching up quarrels, and arranging "truces" in the style described by Napier.[4]

The authors feel that these families are struggling with unconscious wishes for release from this struggle by death. These wishes are defended against via reaction-formation on the family level characterized by the boundless optimism and tension-laden overcooperation. It is not appropriate to explore these underlying wishes, but the consultant must remain aware of these common psychodynamics as he works with the families.

Each family comes to us with a different composition, ethnic background, cultural heritage, and relational history. It has been our experience that those with poor relational histories tend to worsen quickly and appreciably in this context and accordingly have required more time with the liaison team. Families with positive relational histories have done better, but no family prospers in this unique fraternity. Those families in which a member has had previous psychiatric difficulties do the most poorly. To date, one family member, who decompensated from the strain and guilt of the experience, has had to be hospitalized.

Two general family "styles" have had the most difficulties. They fall into the catagories of "over-enmeshed" and "over-distanciated" described by Minuchin.[5] These characterizations fall at the outer edges of the relational spectrum we have seen and *do not* represent the average family in the project. Were this not so, the staff of the project could not possibly persist emotionally in this work. The over-enmeshed family has been previously described by many writers on family psychotherapy, including Wynne,[6] Bowen,[7] and Haley.[8] They experience difficulties in allowing family members emotionally *and* physically to exit from the family system. They have serious difficulties as well in allowing people *into* the family system. Thus, when health care providers will not totally subscribe to the family culture, they are viewed as serious threats. Dissenters from the belief system are punished by ostracism, shunning, or, in the case of health care providers (physical and psychological), by being made to feel that they are causing unbearable psychological pain unnecessarily. By such techniques, great guilt is brought to bear on the medical and nursing staffs. Additionally, enmeshed families have difficulties in allowing the nursing staff to "enter" the family, as they must do, and to assume the intimate parenting role which is so necessary between nurse and bone-marrow transplant patient. More stable families integrate and work with the nurses as a team; less stable, more enmeshed families can not do so. The doublebind occurs when the family is upset by the absence of a solid nurse–patient alliance, absolutely necessary to reduce everyone's anxiety, which the family has blocked from reaching fruition in the first place. It is at these points that liaison consultation is helpful with the nurses, and not as a direct family intervention. With added insight, the nurses can be entirely capable of handling the family–patient–nurse triangular crisis.

The over-distanciated family unit presents another set of problems no less difficult than those described previously. In this type of family, support is not easily obtained by the patient. This tends to inspire an overwhelming sense of abandonment and ultimately, rage in the patient. In the absence of a family unit to express such rage, the patient tends to express rage at the nurses, who are transferential "mother figures" and unconsciously reviewed by the patient as less vital and more expendable than the physicians, hence more appropriate to be objects for one's rage. In the case of one patient, this took the form of attempting to over-control the lives of his closest nurses, wanting to know exactly what they were doing on their days off, when they would be back, what they would wear, etc. When they would return from days off, the patient would "punish" them for abandoning him via passive and active aggression laden with acting out, somatizing, and general negativity for the *exact* amount of time they were gone. All of this anger realistically should have been directed to the actual family, most of whom were usually absent.

In the usual family, one member comes to the hospital. This member is invariably furious at the others, and the fury and schism in the family is perceived by the bone-marrow transplant patient as his or her fault, which increases depression and agitation. This situation has tended to require the liaison consultants to intervene on two levels. The task includes dealing with the family directly to find out what is going on and why they are so conflicted around coming. It also involves helping the nurses understand that they have rights to a life away from the patient, and that the patient's rage is not a result of inappropriate behavior on their part.

REFERENCES

1. Alsobrook HB: Attorney scores concept of M.D. as "Ship Captain" informed consent. Med News (June 5): 23, 1967
2. Kubler-Ross: On Death and Dying. New York, Macmillan, 1970
3. Weisman A: On Dying and Denying. New York, Behavioral, 1972
4. Napier A: Beginning struggles with families. J Marriage Fam Councel 2:3–12, 1976
5. Minuchin S, Montalvo B, Guerney B, Rosmer B, Schumer F: Families of the Slums, an Exploration of their Structure and Treatment. New York, Basic, 1967
6. Wynne L: Maintenance of stereotyped roles in the families of schizophrenics. Arch Gen Psychiatry 1:33–39, 1959
7. Bowen M: A family concept of schizophrenia. *In* Jackson DD (ed): The Etiology of Schizophrenia. New York, Basic, 1960
8. Haley J: Strategies of Psychotherapy. New York, Grune & Stratton, 1963

Charles E. Hollingsworth, Robert Hoffman,
Cynthia Scalzi, and Bernice Sokol

27

Psychosocial Rounds for the Coronary Care Unit

In his chapter on liaison to a coronary care unit (CCU) in his recent book, *Psychological Care of the Physically Ill: A Primer in Liaison Psychiatry*, Strain has outlined the multifaceted approach characteristic of a good liaison psychiatry program to a special medical environment.[1] Rahe has also noted the importance of active participation by liaison psychiatrists in the medical team on the CCU.[2] Other workers, including Cassem and Hackett,[3] Lipowski,[4] Oslfeld et al.,[5] Rosenman,[6] and Theorell and Rahe[7] have discussed the role of personality factors in the development of coronary heart disease. This chapter does not attempt to duplicate their work. In it will be described one very special liaison activity in a university hospital CCU which has been shown to be of great benefit to the staff in helping them work with patients and their families, particularly those families whose members do not recover from their cardiac disease. Parts of this chapter are excerpted from an article entitled "Patient Progress Rounds on a University Cardiology Service."[8]

Psychosocial Patient Progress Rounds is a weekly meeting of representatives of all disciplines associated with the cardiology service devoted to coordinating staff understanding and treatment of all patients, in the interest of providing comprehensive care. Although each patient's clinical status is reviewed, primary attention is given to the

Reprinted with permission from *The American Journal of Psychiatry*, Vol. 134, No. 1 pp 42–44, 1977. Copyright 1977, the American Psychiatric Association.

psychosocial aspects of each case in order to formulate plans for in-hospital management and for long-term care involved in final disposition. It affords an opportunity for the staff to view their patients in the context of the psychosocial milieu in which the patients function, and it serves as a cooperative teaching–learning and consciousness-raising experience for staff, which helps foster esprit de corps. Perhaps most important, it is a multidisciplinary, team enterprise which increases the quality of comprehensive care.

Although this activity is now an integral part of the UCLA Medical Center inpatient cardiology service, it was not included in the unit's original operations. It was developed as one of a series of innovative attempts to respond to a variety of problems not handled adequately by the service's routine procedures. As in most teaching hospitals, UCLA provided the standard assortment of service and teaching functions, including medically oriented conferences and rounds in 1971. While the strictly medical aspects of acute illness were expertly managed, the psychosocial consequences received inadequate attention. Several significant problems were evident. Preeminent among them was a disconcerting readmission rate. When patients who had been readmitted were questioned, it became clear that many had not received adequate instruction on post-discharge care and were confused about activity, diet, and medication. Attempts to rectify this by encouraging the house staff to provide thorough, systematic instructions met with variable success. Some house officers who were interested and motivated prepared their patients well, but many were more involved in the medical aspects of the management of the acute, often life-threatening arrhythmias and hemodynamic events. Hence, they assigned discharge planning lower priority. In fact, the general preoccupation of the medical officers with the medical aspects of acute illness often precluded real understanding of the psychosocial factors, which were given little direct attention. As a result, the very factors which predisposed patients to acquire readmission were frequently overlooked. Of particular concern was the lack of help given to the families in preparing them for the possible consequences of the illness, including sudden death, physical limitation, and emotional reactions to the illness. Even when astute house staff did attempt to deal with the psychosocial concomitants of the patients' illnesses, their efforts were thwarted by the frequent rotation of house officers and the attendant difficulties regarding continuity of care.

The need for a continuing program which depended for reliability on permanent staff became obvious. Therefore, early in 1973, the medical director, head nurse, clinical nurse specialist, and clinical social worker on the unit began to develop educational material around which discharge planning could be focused. In designing the material, the staff explicitly recognized the importance of a health care team which provided adequate medical, nursing, social, and dietary services, as well as psychiatric support. Several brochures were produced and distributed to patients and their families as the basis for scheduled discussions with nurses. An incidental benefit of the implementation of this "teaching program" became evident when patients began questioning their physicians about material in the educational packets and involved house staff in the educational process. As the year progressed, it became clear that communication between members of the health care team was vital to the success of the patient and family educational program. To meet this need, weekly rounds, attended by representatives of all disciplines involved in the health care team, began in March. The status of each patient's clinical course and psychosocial situation was reviewed and information regarding plans for inpatient management and follow-up care was exchanged.

The rounds developed into a weekly 1½-hour meeting of representatives from all disciplines functioning on the coronary care service, including the director and/or codirector of the coronary care service, the medical house staff (who stay for the whole meeting unless they are called for an emergency, in which case they cover for each other so all can be present for at least part of the meeting), the primary care nurses, the liaison psychiatric resident, the clinical social worker, the clinical nurse specialist, the dietitian, the attending physician of the month, undergraduate and graduate students from the various health care disciplines, private M.D.'s, and visiting professionals. The meeting is held at the same hour and day each week in the same large, well-air-conditioned room in which there are enough comfortable chairs and sofas arranged in a large circle to accommodate the 25–30 participants. There is no conference table. The room was chosen after initial meetings in a variety of locations because it provided an atmosphere conducive to the free exchange of information, while minimizing inconvenience and environmental distraction.

The director of the coronary care services begins each session promptly. Each house officer presents a brief vignette of every one of his patients, emphasizing psychosocial factors. Particular attention is paid to the patient's social and family history, his prognosis and predicted convalescence, his coping mechanisms, his understanding of his illness, and discharge plans for follow-up care. House staff may request consultation from one or more of the specialists. Other staff personnel, including the specialists themselves, may suggest consultation, always explaining the rationale for the request. In addition, all staff who have pertinent information are encouraged to share it with the group. This lessens the likelihood that coincidentally obtained but valuable data will be overlooked, and at the same time insures team understanding of the patient from a broader perspective than that held by individual members. After the 20–25 patients on the service, including those who are no longer in the CCU but have been moved onto the wards, have been discussed, follow-up on discharged patients is solicited.

Although it may seem that there is an attempt to cover an inordinate amount of information in a relatively brief period, our experience has been that it is feasible to do meaningful work in the allotted time. Some patients require little time and have few unusual psychosocial difficulties. Others are already known to staff from previous rounds and require only brief follow-up. Therefore, most time is devoted to the relatively small percentage of patients who demand more extensive discussion. The following clinical vignettes serve as useful examples of the kind of work which can be accomplished using this approach.

THE PATIENT WITH MARITAL DISCORD

During patient progress rounds, the nurses requested assistance from the psychiatric liaison consultant to deal with their negative feelings directed towards Mrs. Thompsen, a "demanding patient." The intern knew very little about her family history. The psychiatrist encouraged the intern to find out about this from the patient and her husband. He learned that there had been 30 years of marital discord, the last ten described as "unbearable." Mrs. Thompsen had had emotional problems and Mr. Thompsen had lost his business. In the past, he had suffered from both cardiovascular and cerebrovascular disease. The couple's daughter, who had been sent away to a boarding school as a young child, had never forgiven her parents. Her resentment contributed to the family conflict. In Progress Rounds, the week before the patient was to be discharged, it was pointed out that the family would need domestic help. The social worker contacted the patient's daughter about arranging for household help. She was unreceptive to participating in planning for her mother's discharge. Because domestic help was a pivotal issue for effective post-hospital care, two appointments were held with the daughter to discuss the matter further. During these sessions, the nature of her resistance surfaced. After this very emotional session, the daughter was willing to secure the necessary help. In addition, Mr. Thompsen was offered access to the social worker and arrangements were made for Mrs. Thompsen to receive some psychotherapy at a nearby community mental health center. However, when Mrs. Thompsen left the hospital, she was still demanding and critical of her husband.

Four days after her discharge, her husband collapsed with a myocardial infarction. He was resuscitated by the paramedics and transferred to the UCLA Coronary Care Unit. In Patient Progress Rounds the following week, the intern asked that the social worker and psychiatrist continue their involvement with the family. They found Mr. Thompsen markedly depressed and saw him daily for psychotherapy. By the time he was discharged, arrangements had been made for him to have a housekeeper, a visiting nurse, and daily telephone calls from the social worker during the first two weeks. It was subsequently reported that his wife was much more cooperative and understanding with her husband after he returned home.

THE GRIEVING SPOUSE

During one Psychosocial Patient Progress Rounds session an intern shared his concern about the wife of a critically ill 50-year-old man. The intern requested assistance from the liaison psychiatrist to help her deal with her feelings. It was suggested that the intern refer Mrs. Robinson to the social worker and together they would help her begin the grieving process. It was suggested to the intern that participation in family conferences enables young physicians to learn to help relatives of dying patients cope with their feelings. It was learned that the Robinsons had been totally devoted to each other, and that they had no children. Mrs. Robinson was encouraged to express her feelings of loss. When her husband died she was at his bedside. After his death, she was assured that the social worker and the liaison psychiatrist would be available for continued counseling, and daily phone calls were made to her until several days after the funeral, when she felt she was able to resume various activities. Her friends were also very supportive during this critical time. She later contacted the social worker to request further help, and was referred to a private psychiatrist and to a group therapy program for recently widowed spouses.

THE FAMILY "OVERWHELMED" BY ANXIETY

While Mr. Andrews' case was being reviewed during rounds, the resident requested that the clinical nurse specialist and nursing staff include the patient in the unit's educational program. The impetus for this request appeared to be motivated, at least in part, by his identification with and empathy for a 29-year-old, recently married man who had suffered an extensive myocardial infarction after multiple recent life stresses. After the initial referral, the staff used the rounds as a forum for ongoing communication about the patient's progress, expediting continuity of care as the patient moved from the Coronary Care Unit to the convalescing ward. The staff was able to identify and deal with several problem areas, such as the patient's denial, depression, anger, and feelings of powerlessness. For example, early in the hospital course, he had utilized denial and had been unable to integrate information. Therefore, his educational program was modified to allow him to absorb information at a rate he could handle. In addition, his wife, who was overwhelmed by stress, was given early support and problem solving by the clinical specialist and primary nurse. The various disciplines on the unit coordinated their efforts through the rounds in order to provide special expertise for specific problems. As a result, the staff's anxiety and concern were translated into discrete assistance. In addition, the staff experienced the value of daily communication and teamwork which, in turn, fostered respect and appreciation of the team members for one another.

THE ANGRY PATIENT VERSUS THE ANGRY STAFF

In the case of Mrs. Lewis, members of nursing and house staff learned that the patient had referred to one of the nurses with a racial epithet. The staff became angry, resentful, and defensive. When the patient's hospital course was reviewed at the rounds, staff hostility to the patient was noted by a member of the staff who had not been involved with her. Information regarding the source of staff anger was solicited, and the "rumors" were aired. The angry staff then ventilated their pent-up feelings, which led to an open discussion of ways of dealing with the patient without letting their personal resentment of her behavior interfere with their professional care. In addition, the liaison psychiatrist helped the staff understand that the patient's outburst reflected her insecurity and low self-esteem, and that it could represent displaced frustration rather than genuine antipathy for the target staff member.

Each of the cases cited above demonstrates a multidisciplinary approach to the identification and management of patients' problems. They also reflect cooperative learning experiences for staff, involving the value of thorough assessment of a patient's psychosocial milieu, the availability of hospital and community resources to provide special services for in- and out-patient care, the variety of techniques of consultation pertinent to the provision of comprehensive care, and the modalities of therapy for families in mourning. The rounds provide an opportunity for patients to be individually evaluated in the interest of comprehensive care. This is in contradistinction to the kind of conceptualization of patients as cases fostered by traditional medical rounds, which often focus on lab and x-ray data, abnormal physical findings (i.e., physiological pathology), while de-emphasizing if not entirely neglecting the person's psychosocial system. As a result, the entire staff is able to deal with people who happen to be sick and who have a variety of complex problems in conjunction with their illnesses. The benefits for the patients and their families are self-evident.

Equally significant are the benefits for staff. Progress rounds help prepare young physicians to deal with patients in the real world with more of the kind of understanding often lamented as having vanished with the "bedside manner" of the old-fashioned family physician, always valued by patients and lately reemerging among enlightened young doctors. The team approach that is so vital to the ongoing teaching of all members of the team, presents the patient not only as an individual with an illness requiring medical care and treatment, but also as a person whose fears, prejudices, and attitudes toward his illness and prescribed treatment have been conditioned by his background of experiences and his environment. Contributions of social and personal data are provided by the team members in order to better understand the patient in the context of his total situation. Other educational benefits accrue from Progress Rounds as well. The staff learns how to use consultants appropriately, and how to obviate the necessity for consultation by acquiring some additional expertise from their dealings with the consultants, since all consultations are oriented to teaching as much as to patient care.

In summary, the Psychosocial Patient Progress Rounds provide a unique tool in a teaching hospital which facilitates the reintegration of humanistic considerations into highly specialized, technologically sophisticated, but all-too-often emotionally impoverished modern medicine, through teamwork. It is an innovative, practical tool for improving the quality of both health care and teaching in a hospital setting which is not utilized by the vast majority of medical centers with which the authors, or any of their associates, are acquainted. This belief has been reinforced by experiences at a variety of formal and informal professional gatherings across the country, where information about this program was shared. The authors believe that this activity could serve as a model for the development of similar activities at other hospitals to "help the helpers."

REFERENCES

1. Strain JJ, Grossman S: Psychological care of the medically ill: a primer in liaison psychiatry. New York, Appleton–Century Crofts, 1975

2. Rahe R: A liaison psychiatrist on the coronary care unit. *In* Pasnau RO: Consultation-Liaison Psychiatry. New York, Grune & Stratton, 1975, pp 115–122

3. Cassem NH, Hackett TP: Psychiatric consultation in a coronary care unit. Ann Intern Med 75:9–14, 1971

4. Lipowski ZJ: Review of consultation psychiatry and psychosomatic medicine. I. General principles. Psychosom Med 29:153–171, 1967. II. Clinical aspects. Psychosom Med 29:201–225, 1967. III. Theoretical issues. Psychosom Med 30:395–422, 1968

5. Oslfeld A, Lebovits BZ, Shekelle RB, et al: A perspective study of the relationship between personality and coronary heart disease. J Chron Dis 17:265–276, 1974

6. Rosenman RH: Emotional factors in coronary heart disease. Postgrad Med 42:165–172, 1967

7. Theorell T, Rahe RH: Psychosocial factors and myocardial infarction: I. An inpatient study in Sweden. J Psychosom Res 15:25–31, 1971

8. Hollingsworth CE, Hoffman R, Scalzi C, Sokol B: Patient progress rounds on a university hospital cardiology service. Am J Psychiatry 134(1):42–44, 1977

PART VI

Conclusion

Conclusion

We have attempted to write a book that focuses on the living—the living patients and the living family, as well as the caregivers, both professional and nonprofessional. What began as a project describing a single family in a state of profound disturbance from a series of tragic illness and loss, developed into an exploration of the various aspects of bereavement as it is encountered by the health professions.

We have stressed the importance of the physician's role in informing families of the death of a member and the importance of support during the early mourning period. Prevention of the more pathological mourning states and initiation of the grief response is the primary goal of the professional in the acute phase.

We have attempted to cover some of the theoretical bases of direct clinical pertinance, especially the parents' response to the death of a child, a child's response to the death in the family, and the grieving spouse. In addition, we have looked at some special areas of grieving, including response to the birth of a handicapped child and grief following abortion.

We have looked at various ways of helping the family in mourning. Visiting and working with bereaved families and spouses, the role of religion and culture, and the role of psychotherapy have been explored.

We have included some chapters that describe the role of the liaison psychiatrist who works closely with the medical team, with the ultimate responsibility for patient and family care, and described some of the difficulties of such a role. Some promising programs for helping the helpers have been developed, and other programs will be devised in the future. It may be that the mainstream of psychiatry in the years to come will lie in the area of comprehensive medical care and liaison with the rest of medicine. It is an appropriate area of concern to be included in a book about families in mourning. In recognizing the personal, intense feelings of sorrow and grief experienced by a family, we are reminded of our own mortality and finiteness. The health care professionals who are involved with the care of critically ill individuals and their families face extreme emotional and physical stress. A major role of liaison psychiatric intervention is to provide ways for dealing with this stress, and opening up the lines of communication and support from them to their patients and to their families.

This book is an attempt to focus on the multidisciplinary aspect of this important work, as well as upon the need for comprehensive and continuous care over time. For some families, it is only necessary to assure that the community or religious support systems are activated. For others a counseling or psychological approach is best. As C. G. Jung wrote:

> I am not addressing myself to the happy professors of faith, but to those many people for whom the light has gone out, the mystery has faded, and God is dead. For most of them there is no going back, and one does not know either whether going back is the better way. To gain an understanding of religious matters, probably all that is left us today is the psychological approach. That is why I take these thought-forms that have become historically fixed, try to melt them down again and pour them into moulds of immediate experience.[1]

The holistic approach to patient care requires an appreciation of all of the facets of a family's experience and the sensitive awareness of one's own abilities, limits, and vulnerabilities. We hope that this book will be a useful volume for all of those disciplines involved in the humane approach to health care delivery.

REFERENCE

1. Jung CG: Psychology and religion. *In* Psychology and Religion: West and East. In Collected Works, Princeton, N.J., Princeton University Press, 1969, Vol. II

Index